WHAT MAKES YOUR TEAM TICK?

*Taking Your Team
to the Next Level of
Superior Performance*

LONNIE MORELOCK

DEDICATION

This book is dedicated to all those who have selflessly taken the time to teach, train, and mentor me. Your wisdom, knowledge, love, caring, and belief in me have all come together to make my life, career, and this book a possibility.

For those who have passed on, I look forward to meeting you again in Heaven. May your legacy live forever through the pages of this book.

For the people who continue to help shape my life, your never-ending guidance, love, and support have a very special place in my heart.

GET IN TOUCH

🌐 Morelockmotivational.com

✉ Lonnie@morelockmotivational.com

TABLE OF CONTENTS

FOREWORD

Over the last 28 years, I have owned and operated Selby's Soil Erosion Control (SSEC), starting from one truck in 1995 in Northern California to now becoming the largest hydroseeding and erosion control contractor covering the Pacific Northwest with an office in Idaho.

My father was a great inspiration to me growing up. He told me there was nothing I couldn't do if I put my mind to it. In my younger years, I was fearless and determined. On top of running my business, I was a committed rock climber with many achievements, like conquering the face of Half Dome. As a mountaineer, I climbed the highest peaks on five continents, sometimes taking up to a month to reach the summit. Unfortunately, I had to retire from climbing at age 27 due to injuries.

I first met Lonnie in the fall of 2001. He was a project superintendent for Kiewit Pacific. His background began when he was an equipment operator in 1980, right out of high school, at the age of 18. He worked hard at learning to operate all types of mass-grading heavy equipment and then became a grade setter at Teichert Construction Co. in 1991. He moved to Kiewit Pacific Co. in 1992, where he quickly moved up in the company to make civil grading foreman in 1993. He then went on to join the Kiewit Pacific management team, venturing out to take a salaried position in 2000 as a field superintendent.

Back to the fall of 2001. I was still considered a kid in the industry as I was in my mid-twenties and mostly dealing with owners, inspectors, or superintendents in their forties. I knew of the reputation of the great Lonnie Morelock and that you better hold his pace or get out of his way. He ran the tightest crews around, and most owners or owner's reps requested him and his teams for that reason. Kiewit and SSEC were both contracted by the "take no bullshit" toughest owner's representatives I have ever known.

Robert Parish worked with Lonnie on a project in Lincoln, California, called Twelve Bridges. Obviously, he and Lonnie hit it off instantly. They were of the same mindset, driving over-expectations and pushing everyone around them to the limits, all the while still demanding and expecting the greatest quality of work. I was already intimidated by Rob, but at that point, I had proved to him that I was capable, and he seemed to like me. By that, I mean he didn't yell at me like he did to most! LOL!

Then entered Lonnie Morelock. I was so intimidated by him. I mean, there was this giant of a man who looked like he could crush me with one hand. In the weekly job meetings, I would sit in the back and not say a word or cause any waves as I listened and watched intently while Rob and Lonnie laid out the workload and plan for the week.

Then, an emergency brought us all together. A huge hillside, several hundred feet tall, became a major landslide, covering the finished house pads below as a massive storm headed our way. Several creeks and protected wetlands were very nearby. Lonnie, Rob, and the crews worked insane hours all weekend to fix the repair and rebuild the hillside before the first significant incoming rain storm was predicted to arrive in Northern California.

We knew we would be inspected by the Water Quality Control Board (WQCB) the day after the storm passed. If we discharged muddy water into the creeks and protected wetlands, we could incur massive fines; worse, they might shut the job down.

My crews and I worked directly behind Lonnie as his dozers got to finished grade, hydroseeding the slopes right behind him. We all worked late into the night, well past midnight, using mobile light towers and light plants to see what we were doing. We finished exactly one and a half hours before the storm hit. Although the rainstorm packed one hell of a punch, we passed our WQCB inspection with flying colors.

I had finally earned Lonnie's respect, which was a very proud moment in my life. Who would have known that Rob and Lonnie would become big teddy bears and "best friends" later in life and that, to this very day, we all would stay in touch?

After the Twelve Bridges Project, I worked beside Lonnie on several other major mass-grading projects, including Whitney Ranch, sewer treatment plants, water treatment plants, and many more, and we became great friends. In 2010, Kiewit shipped Lonnie, by then a senior project manager, to British Columbia to help fix their problem child: the Port Mann Highway.

I lost track of Lonnie for many years as he continued his project management career with Kiewit, specializing in assisting teams on problem projects. But then the next emergency happened that brought us back together, and this one was of epic proportions.

In February of 2017, Lake Oroville—backed up by Oroville Dam in Northern California and one of the largest earth-fill dams in the United States, was at full capacity due to heavy rainfall in the region. This led to the failure of the main emergency spillway. It literally undermined and collapsed half of this concrete structure. There was so much water that the secondary emergency spillway overflowed, washing trees, soil, and debris into the Feather River and prompting the evacuation of more than 180,000 people living downstream of the lake. If the secondary spillway failed, as experts were predicting, a 30-foot wall of water would have rushed through the town of Oroville and into the valley below.

As soon as the torrential rains stopped, the Department of Water Resources (DWR) sprang into action, hiring emergency contractors, including my company SSEC, to clean up and patch the immediate damage while engineers went to work designing a permanent fix.

Months later, Kiewit Pacific Co. was awarded the contract for this multi-year undertaking to build a new spillway and reinforce the secondary emergency spillway. Of course, they hired SSEC to partner with them on the project.

On my first day on the job, I was very pleased to see that Kiewit had brought Lonnie back to California to help manage the project. Every Tuesday for nearly two years, Lonnie and I would drive the entire project, devising a "think outside the box" erosion control plan to meet the stringent requirements for DWR's approval.

This was a massive undertaking as the project had multiple on-site rock quarries and heavy earthmoving equipment going in every direction to build the necessary infrastructure to keep the cranes and structures working—which were everywhere. Nearly 300 acres of steep mountainous terrain were exposed. It amazed me every Tuesday how orchestrated and organized Lonnie and his team were. They just ticked like a synchronized watch. As we were brainstorming together and highlighting plans in the field, Lonnie's telephone was constantly going off, informing him of everything from dumpster deliveries to water truck locations, labor crews always asking questions, expediting dozer operations, crane locations, and on and on.

It was insane how Lonnie could hold it all together while working long hours 6-7 days a week. Everyone involved in the project held their mark, and it was completed ahead of schedule.

Lonnie let me know that this would be his last job for Kiewit. He wanted to follow his dream and start his own consulting company, Morelock Motivational, focusing on construction field leadership development.

Following his retirement from Kiewit, Lonnie came to me for business advice a few months later. We had lunch, and he had a detailed list of questions about running a business. He left that lunch with me as his first client.

Shortly afterward, Lonnie started training several of my foremen on their field management skills and overall efficiency. He would observe them for a day without interfering or really saying anything; then, in the following days, he would show them how to be better leaders and improve teamwork and leadership efficiency.

In the construction world, teaching foremen is a pretty intimidating situation. I remember how the first foreman we chose for Lonnie to work with said, "Really!! He doesn't even know our line of work. What's he going to teach me? I've been doing this for 15 years." Several weeks later, that same foreman thanked me because Lonnie had taught him so much and brought out leadership talent and skills that this foreman never knew he had. After that, the rest of the foremen got in line quickly, begging to go through his course, and it didn't end there. Lonnie stayed in touch with them months later to check on their ongoing progress.

I then brought Lonnie in to speak in front of the entire company as a motivational speaker. Most guys rolled their eyes when I announced that we were going to have a meeting at Top Golf and a guest speaker. But Lonnie somehow got through to them, and everyone in the room left totally pumped up and ready to work on improving themselves with greater pride in the company.

Fast forward several years and SSEC's safety record wasn't great, with over 10 accidents in just one year. We decided to make a new, permanent position for a safety officer in the company. Before this, each project manager had handled the safety of his crews. We had in-house, the perfect guy to hold this position, Mike. He had been a foreman for the company for nearly 15 years and knew every job safety requirement needed. The crews respected him.

The only problem was that we needed to develop a plan to train Mike on how to become a senior manager. I called Lonnie, who had already trained Mike to be a better foreman and leader a year prior, and said, "We need to develop a plan for Mike to take his leadership skills and abilities to the next level."

Lonnie jumped right in, working on and off over the next few months with Mike to develop him for the new position. Mike drank the training up, and he and Lonnie had fun doing it together. Mike has gone on to become an awesome manager and still calls Lonnie for advice.

Lonnie continued to speak, coach, and train many large companies' top performers. Every time I called him, he was working hard and trying to keep up with the demand, sharing his leadership training, team-building style, and real-world experience with the construction industry. He was living his passion, building better people and better leaders. His trainees were happier for it, and their work environment and performance improved greatly.

A month ago, I got a call from Lonnie. In Lonnie fashion, he said, "Jay, I wrote my first book on *How to Make Your Team Tick*, and I want you to write the foreword." First off, I was completely blown away. *How does he have time to write a book, and what's a foreword?*

I laughed out loud, but after a few days of hearing what he said, I realized his next passion project made total sense.

There's just not enough of Lonnie to go around, and this book solves that problem. I cannot tell you what an honor it is to introduce this amazing book from a truly great man and one of my best friends.

Enjoy the read,
Jay Selby
Founder, SSEC

INTRODUCTION

*W*hat Makes Your Team Tick!?

I know that is a pretty vague question.

But I want you to stop for a moment and think about the awesome teams you've had the blessed opportunity to have been a part of in your lifetime.

Maybe you are a member of a very successful, high-performing team. It could be any type of team: a construction project team, a sports team, a management team, an industry production team, or a scientific team. I'm talking about a team of any size, shape, or color performing "OFF THE CHARTS," or, as you will hear me say many times throughout this book, one that is achieving Performance Above & Beyond.

It's been a mystery to me for a while—especially in the construction industry—that regularly ignores anything having to do with touchy-feely emotions or having the hard conversations about what people are really thinking about. But have you ever stopped and thought about what it is that makes your team so special?

That's what we're about to uncover in these pages.

- What are the inner workings of a superstar team?
- How do you get there?
- What adversities must you overcome?
- How do you get everyone on the team on board, or as I like to say, "on the same page?"
- What do you do to get every team member to set their egos aside and give their all to support the team?

All great questions.

Before I started coaching organizations on how to find the answers, I had to find the answers myself. All I could think about was *what makes a successful team tick?* Around me, I could see all sorts of teams that weren't ticking.

Before I tell you how I got the answer, let me give you a little more information on my background that caused me to be so obsessed and not stop until I found out.

WE PUT THE "FUN" IN DYSFUNCTIONAL

I grew up in what can only be described as a dysfunctional family. Yes, there were many good times and memories, but way more were not-so-good.

I learned early on that being part of a good team gave me a place of refuge. A solid group of individuals giving their all and trying to be the best they could be was where I could fit in and be a positive collaborator. This became my happy place!

I didn't know what would happen when I joined a team. It was an unknown adventure and a positive side effect.

2

I started out just wanting to have some fun and forget about the problems at home. My groups took many forms. Sometimes, all the local kids came together to form neighborhood baseball teams that would play all day long, or we would have weekend tackle football games at the local park or school.

I was an observer, learning that putting the best players in the right positions usually meant victory! Everyone had to do their part to be a contributing member of the team and help the other teammates perform at their best levels by encouraging, motivating, and leading. The feeling of it all was incredible, and it took the place of the heartache and mayhem waiting at home.

As I grew up, I became a part of organized sports teams, like high school football, basketball, and track. I learned the power of a well-balanced team, the power of training, and of improving skills and abilities. I saw and felt the overwhelming power of motivation, encouragement, and recognition—all ingredients that led to being part of winning teams.

When I started my construction career right out of high school, I realized even more the significance of the power of a team and what an awesome team could accomplish.

MY FIRST BIG PROJECT

Becoming part of an earthmoving spread of heavy equipment, aka "big iron," on my first big project, Warm Springs Dam in Healdsburg, California (now Lake Sonoma), was a real eye-opener.

What a team of earthmovers, working together in perfect unison, could accomplish in a day was absolutely amazing. Receiving training by men who were the best of the best at what they did quickly taught me how good on-the-job training could improve your skills and abilities to achieve remarkable results.

The flip side was learning how negative impacts could affect the team's overall performance. In those situations, nothing could go right. The entire team was screwed up "like a homemade radio" (a favorite saying of mine borrowed from a great friend and colleague).

Learning how to make a negative into a positive became an obsession. The more I observed the inner workings of a team, the more I learned how to get a dysfunctional team to click and fire on all cylinders to overcome adversity and achieve what was once perceived as impossible results.

I made it my mission to figure out how to build a group of people to be one team and combine all their individual skills, talents, and abilities. I studied the team to unravel what makes them tick. Then, I took it a step further by bringing people together to work in unison and become a supercharged, high-performing team. What I learned during those years is the essence of this book.

What Makes Your Team Tick? explores and explains what can and will help your team consistently perform at high levels of production and achievement.

From childhood to high school to heavy equipment operator to craft foreman to superintendent to senior project manager, my experiences over my entire construction career have given me the opportunity to lead amazing teams, and they have led me to my passion. It is the passion of training individuals to be the best they can be and, in the process, helping them to build winning teams.

Along the way, I have learned to evaluate and answer the question, "What Makes Your Team Tick?" It is my hope that this book will help you discover the same thing—that it will give you the tools, skills, abilities, and knowledge to lead dynamic teams of your own!

LET'S MAKE IT HAPPEN!

CHAPTER 1

THE ART OF ABSOLUTE TEAMWORK

"Create an environment where people can take risks.
If everything has to be brilliant from the word 'go,'
you're never gonna get off the ground."
—Paul Hewson, aka Bono

Let's start off with the first question you are probably asking yourself: "What the hell is Absolute Teamwork?" What does that even mean?

In my world, the world of heavy construction, it means a group of craft individuals working together in the field in perfect unison. It is one concise unit, synchronized like a Rolex watch. As you read through this book, you will hear me talk a lot about the Rolex watch. No, I don't have one YET, but someday, I plan to own one to remind me of where its significance has led me.

If you study the Rolex watch and how it was first made, you will see that its inner functions and chronometric precision are absolutely meticulous. Every mechanism works perfectly together with

5

the other; they are 100% in sync. The development of the Rolex watch came about due to the pursuit of absolute perfection. Even over many years, the time the Rolex watch keeps is as close to perfection as possible. The inner workings of the watch are an example of Absolute Teamwork. The results are flawless execution.

THE CATERPILLAR 657—"THE ROLEX WATCH OF EARTHMOVERS"

When I started working in heavy construction, I quickly learned what Absolute Teamwork meant.

When I began running a Caterpillar 657 Multi-Engine Scraper, I thought I'd died and gone to heaven. *What a blast! I am actually getting paid to run this awesome piece of earthmoving machinery?* At 19 years old, those were my thoughts, and that was a big friggin' deal!

Through the training and mentoring of some of the best scraper operators in the business, I understood what these miraculous machines could do. When a team works together, two 657 operators running in perfect synchronization is beautiful to behold.

To better familiarize you with the features of these machines, let me introduce you to them before I go off on a tangent. These 657 Scrapers are called "push-pull" scrapers. They have a bail on the front that lowers over the stinger, aka the hook, on the back. When they enter the excavation pit, the back scraper "hooks up" to the front scraper and pushes it until it is loaded. When the front scraper is fully loaded and pulls out of the ground, the rear scraper lets up the slack on the bail and connects the bail to the stinger in the back of the front scraper. The front scraper pulls the rear scraper until it is loaded. The rear scraper then pulls out of the ground, and the increase in momentum causes the back scraper to shift to a higher gear; the back scraper jumps forward and unhooks the bail from the front scraper. They then separate, and both haul ass to the fill area or the dump site.

When a team is in sync, applying the correct power when needed, and working the cut correctly, the machines look like they are literally "dancing" together. We will talk more about dancing later in this book.

Picture 24 of these 657 Scrapers working together as 12, 2-person teams in perfect synchronization. You can literally move mountains in a day. It is INCREDIBLE.

That's one example of what I call Absolute Teamwork.

Let's look at another component that will help your team reach the goal of Absolute Teamwork.

PERFORMANCE–ABOVE & BEYOND

Performance Above & Beyond is the exact saying I have carried throughout my career. I know it sounds like a corny cliché or BS lingo, but when I share with you how that saying came to mind, you will understand its significance.

Early on, as I was undertaking my own personal construction leadership development, I studied fighter pilots. I was always in awe of not only their bravery but at the sheer magnitude of what it takes to become one. Fighter pilots go through rigorous training involving countless hours of practice and testing and strain the limits of their physical endurance just to get to sit down in that cockpit. Then, they close the canopy centered behind the joystick, hit the afterburners, and soar seamlessly into the sky. Unbelievable.

They push their fighter jets to performance levels above and beyond what even they could have imagined.

This brings to mind Brigadier General Chuck Yeager, arguably one of the greatest jet pilots and test pilots of all time. He wasn't scared of anything but relied on his gut, instincts, God-given talent, and abilities to take his newly designed jets to performance levels the engineers didn't believe were attainable.

Breaking the sound barrier, something never achieved before, is the epitome of Performance Above & Beyond.

I have used the fighter pilot analogy in my construction team operations and in coaching the performance of construction project leaders. And I have wondered *what does it take to get a team of individuals to perform above and beyond?* How can a project operation hit the equivalent of the afterburners of the Bell X-1 Rocket (the test jet that Chuck broke the sound barrier in) to take the team to a performance level never believed to be achievable, aka "Performance Above & Beyond?"

By the grace of God, I have seen some great team members. The awesome talent I have been blessed to work with takes individuals and teams to that distinct level time and time again.

That's what this book is about. That's what Continuous Improvement is about. That's what Performance Above & Beyond is about. That's what Absolute Teamwork is about—getting to that next level.

The concept is so simple.

Couple the hard work of Continuous Improvement with achieving Performance Above & Beyond, and that dynamic duo will create Absolute Teamwork. That is the sum of all the parts. That is the goal.

No matter the structure of your team, whether you are running an operations team, leadership team, or a different model, Absolute Teamwork is getting to the highest level of achievement possible.

That is the "holy grail" to success on any construction project—to be the absolute best you can be.

That's just the tip of the iceberg. Keep reading for more about managing and supporting your team exceptionally because I haven't even gotten started.

When an entire team of builders comes together, whether it's civil grading teams moving mountains, drainage teams laying underground piping, structures teams building concrete spillways, treatment plants, or skyscrapers, paving teams building brand new asphalt roads, etc., working in perfect unison as one team unit, completely organized, coordinated, and performing at the top of their game, the magic happens.

Performance Above & Beyond is achieved when production levels are off the charts, "impossible" schedule deadlines are "smoked," and a magnificent piece of infrastructure is left in its wake. This is the epitome of Absolute Teamwork. To be a part of it on any construction project is the pinnacle of being a builder.

I have been there many times, and the feeling is fantastic. I have been blessed to have led many of those teams, and the thrill of watching the team grow and come together and helping people learn and grow in their careers is one of fulfillment that cannot be explained by all the words in *Webster's Dictionary*.

Let me try to sum it up through this quote by the great Vince Lombardi, famous leader and former head coach of the Green Bay Packers. He shared these sentiments with his team in 1959, before his team went on to achieve greatness: "But I firmly believe that the greatest fulfillment for all we hold dear is that moment when we have worked our heart out for a good cause, and lie down on the field of battle, exhausted but victorious!"

But just what is the secret sauce for Absolute Teamwork? How do we Make It Happen? How does it happen on any team in any industry, sporting or motorsport event, or other type of team? That is where I am going to take you in this book. You will join me on a path that focuses on intense training, Continuous Improvement, striving for Performance Above & Beyond, and finally, reaching the coveted goal of Absolute Teamwork.

Sit back, grab a chair, and let me take you on an adventure you may have never gone on before. It's an adventure leading to personal growth, pride, and an immeasurable sense of accomplishment.

I KNOW YOU'RE GONNA LOVE IT!

CHAPTER 2

BEING THE LEADER

"Before you are a leader, success is all about growing yourself. When you become a leader, success is all about growing others."
—Jack Welch

Leader. Leadership. Probably two of the most misunderstood words in the human language.

What is a leader?

What does it mean to "be a leader"? What the hell does leadership stand for anyway? Can any specific definition really be followed? There are lots of good questions with very few real answers concerning this topic. "LEADER" is a HUGE WORD.

Whenever I get stuck on a word, I always jump to Google, hit the *Webster's Dictionary* icon, and enter the word in the search. Simple and easy.

Well, sort of . . .

I KEPT IT IN MY POCKET

Since I'd barely made it through high school, my vocabulary was not the greatest. I initially survived on my pocket dictionary, kept in reach at all times.

Then, I graduated to a thesaurus when I could find one or a quick call to a more educated friend. But over the years, that thesaurus was my go-to vocabulary increaser!

When Google came along, it continued to ease my education. Fortunately, I never really had a problem with slang vocabulary. The construction industry helped me out with this thoroughly! However, descriptive slang can be an issue when giving a presentation, especially a motivational one that winds me all up like a spinning top! Sometimes, I needed to use REAL, gritty, everyday words that might be frowned upon but that everyone understands.

Regardless, *Merriam-Webster* tells us that the definition of the word "leader" can be broken up into two pieces. "Lead" means to lead or to "guide on a way especially by going in advance" and "to direct operations, activity, or performance."[1] Yes, I realize that's a little vague. "To guide someone or something along the way" is a little better or more specific. "Leader" is defined as "a person who has commanding authority or influence."[2] Wow. That seems a little dictatorial. Finally, "Leadership" is defined as "the capacity to lead, the act or instance of leading."[3]

---

1   "Lead Definition & Meaning." Merriam-Webster. Accessed November 21, 2024. https://www.merriam-webster.com/dictionary/lead.

2   "Leader Definition & Meaning." Merriam-Webster. Accessed November 16, 2024. https://www.merriam-webster.com/dictionary/leader.

3   "Leadership Definition & Meaning." Merriam-Webster. Accessed November 16, 2024. https://www.merriam-webster.com/dictionary/leadership.

I have my own definition. Being a leader means "to take people in the direction you want them to go, then doing all you can to help them get there." And I really mean *all* you can do!

> *I grew up reading about great leaders in history. Good and bad. I focused on the good and great leaders because that was the pinnacle I wanted to achieve.*

I had absolutely no desire or inkling to be a bad leader. I wanted to be like George Washington, leading the Continental Army across the Delaware on Christmas night to eventually win the first battle with the British Empire during the American Revolution. I would marvel at how he could get his men to follow him through the bitter cold of winter with little food, provisions, and ammunition, going up against one of the greatest fighting forces in history.

After immersing myself in Washington, I studied the leadership of Abraham Lincoln for hours. He guided the nation through the Civil War and the abolition of slavery, putting the entire country on a new path of freedom. I often wondered *how is he able to get "like-minded" people to follow him?*

Once I'd read enough history on these two leaders, I moved on to modern-day biographies, spending countless hours reading about great sports teams' leaders/coaches who had taken their teams to the pinnacle of success in their respective leagues.

I liked the NFL coaches John Madden, Bill Walsh, and Jimmy Johnson. But by far, my favorite was Vince Lombardi, the legendary NFL coach of the Green Bay Packers. He had such a unique leadership style and character. I loved how he led and motivated his teams, always focusing on the positive and finding the greatness that each and every one of his team members had within them.

As I entered the workforce, I learned firsthand the effect of a good leader or the dramatic, negative effect of a bad leader. There were and are so many examples to refer to.

In addition to studying the great leaders in history and sports, I was blessed to have worked under some great leaders whose mentoring and tutelage got me to where I am today.

THE POWER OF EXPECTATIONS

One of the most astonishing discoveries in my growth as a leader was learning about and understanding the power of expectations. Right out of the gate, I urge you to make your expectations "crystal clear." By that, I mean let your team or "your people" know exactly what you expect of them. I do this regularly, and it's a Game-Changer.

I have worked for many bosses over the years who never really shared with our team what they expected or wanted to accomplish.

Numerous times, I can remember getting chewed out because I did something I was not supposed to do, even though I had never been told that what I was doing was considered wrong. I used to wonder to myself, *why doesn't he just tell me exactly what he wants? I can't read minds.*

I've always believed in my heart there must be a better way to lead. I can tell you that there is.

I am a quote guy. I love great quotes. One of my favorites concerning expectations came from none other than John Steinbeck. His quote was, "It is the nature of man to rise to greatness if greatness is expected of him." WOW. That was and is powerful to me.

I developed this quote further. Here is how it played out.

THE TURNAROUND

As I was gathering more leadership experience under my belt, I was sent to a project completely upside down, severely behind schedule, and that was losing massive amounts of money. When I arrived on site, I saw that the team was about as beaten down and dejected as they could be. I had never seen a group so downtrodden. Jaws were on the ground, and everyone was worn out and mentally exhausted. The looks on their faces told me that a good many were also probably preoccupied by the possibility of their careers being in the toilet.

As I drove to my condo that night, I thought, *how can I immediately get through to this team? I've got to turn their negativity into positivity as quickly as possible.*

They needed to know, right up front, what I expected of them going forward. But then I hit on something even more monumental: *What did they expect of me?* I still get chills when I think about this moment in time that changed everything.

That night, I sat down at the kitchen table and made a short list of my expectations. The next day was my first staff meeting with the entire group. I was nervous as hell. This specific assignment was one of the greatest challenges I had ever faced as a senior project manager. But the words of United States Navy Admiral David Farragut, "Damn the torpedoes. Full speed ahead," rang through my ears.

I'd called the meeting for early afternoon to give me more time to build up my courage. When I walked into the conference room, I could hear my heartbeat, and it was loud! There was absolute, deafening silence. I kept saying to myself, *I'm cool. I'm cool. I got this. Piece of cake* . . . as my stomach turned, and I thought any minute I would throw up.

Instead, I calmly introduced myself and said, "I am going to start by making myself crystal clear." (I was thinking of the movie *A Few*

15

Good Men with Tom Cruise and Jack Nicholson when Jack asks Tom, "Are we *clear*?" and Tom responds, "Crystal.")

I continued, "So there is no question or gray area of any kind; I want to share with you my expectations for this team going forward. This is what I expect from you, day in and day out. Nothing more. You live up to these expectations on a daily basis, and I assure you we will be all good. Better than good. Are we clear . . . crystal clear?!" I got zero reaction. The team was so stoic I thought *maybe they can't handle the truth*?!

Then, I went on to share my specific expectations. They were as follows:

1. Nobody Gets Hurt
2. Build the Highest Quality of Work Achievable
3. Maintain Absolute Integrity
4. Always Exhibit Professional Performance
5. Negative Attitudes Are UNACCEPTABLE
6. Practice EXTREME Housekeeping
7. Knowing Your Daily Cost Is Mandatory
8. Never Start an Operation Without a Well-Thought-Out Plan
9. Treat Every Piece of Equipment You Use Like You Bought It with Your Own Money
10. Set Difficult Goals and Then Work Your Heart out to Achieve Them
11. Treat Everyone on Your Team with the Highest Levels of Dignity, Honor, and Respect
12. Believe in the Impossible, Never Say Can't, and Give Your Absolute Best EVERY DAY

When I finished, it was silent again. All I could hear was my own soft breathing. There were no remarks, comments, or questions from the group. Just utter silence. I was, of course, thinking, *damn, this is going to be a tough nut to crack*. Then, I noticed a large grease board close by.

As you get deeper into this book, you will learn that I have a real affinity for grease boards. They are great friends of mine. I love them, and they love me!

I turned to the team and said, "Okay, now that you have heard my expectations, I am going to turn my attention to this beautiful grease board." There were plenty of dry-erase pens and lots of colors for everyone. *Sssswwweeeett*! For a moment, I think they all thought I had lost my mind. I continued, "I have given each of you a printed copy of my expectations. Now, I want you to tell me exactly what YOU EXPECT OF ME because if I am going to lead you, if we, as a team, are going to turn this job around, I have to know what you expect of me. I promise you; I will move Heaven and Earth to meet your expectations! I mean, how can I share my expectations of you yet not expect you to share your expectations of me?"

The response from this group blew me away. Eyes lit up, color returned to faces, and I saw faint smiles forming on many lips. Immediately, a project engineer stood up and said without hesitation, "I have been on this job for three years, and never has a manager or supervisor asked me what I expected of them!"

I replied, "Well, it is my pleasure to give you the honor of being the first one on the grease board." I grabbed a pen and asked her, "What is your expectation?" She uttered, "I want to be more involved with the schedule so I can better understand my role." Then, like an earthen dam bursting and water rushing out, the entire team joined in. One after another, they all shouted out answers. A guy with close-cropped hair and a raspy voice jumped up and yelled, "I need to be more involved with the whole change order process. How can I price something I know nothing about?!" More people spoke up, and I listened and wrote.

I was getting writer's cramp as I jotted down their words as fast as I could, and the grease board filled up. One expectation after another fired at me like baseballs from a pitching machine. When we finished, there was, without a doubt, a new feeling in the room. I knew instantly I had gained this team's trust. As a team, we had our expectations of each other and our first path forward.

> *If you have never shared your expectations of your team and asked them to share their expectations of you, I highly recommend that you give it a try.*

IT IS POWERFUL STUFF. AN ICE BREAKER. A TEAM BUILDER. A MOTIVATOR.

THERE IS ONLY "1" OF YOU

When my mind drifts back to my high school days, I always think of the guys I used to play sports with. I played with really great athletes—way better than I ever was, although I thought I was a pretty damn good receiver at one point in my high school football career. I actually earned the nickname "Freddie B.," after Fred Biletnikoff, a famous wide receiver for the then-dominant Oakland Raiders. But as good as I thought I was, I never got to the level of my peers. Jesse was an awesome running back. Luis was the crème de la crème of quarterbacks.

In basketball, which I also loved to play, team camaraderie was my favorite part. But I could never shoot like Dwight. He was friggin' awesome and could hit three-pointers like no other.

Although I could run like the wind in track and loved pole vaulting, 100m hurdles, and triple jump, I could never equal Noel's ability—my hero in the track world.

Finally, in baseball, possibly my best sport concerning my overall ability—despite wearing glasses—even though I could hit, catch long balls on the run in left field, and had a stint as a pitcher, I would never be as good as Johnny.

Comparing myself to the people I thought I would never beat used to bother me greatly. *Why can't I do what they do?* I practiced my heart out and worked my butt off . . . but never could quite measure up. Over time, I realized these young men were just better athletes than me, and that was that. They were who they were, and I was who I was. There was only one of them, and there was only one of me.

Period!

FOREMAN WEIRD-OH!

Let's fast-forward to when I first became a foreman. Before I dive completely in, I need to tell you that later in the book, you will learn how I got the nickname Taz in my early leadership experiences. Unfortunately, a problem sparking that nickname metastasized into another issue I was confronted with—which I will also explain.

> *For now, all you need to know is that the first project I was assigned to as foreman showed me a vision that changed my life and how I work with teams today.*

One day, from out of nowhere, I "saw" the project before me literally open up before my eyes. I was truly astounded by what I could see. Before any haul road changes took shape, major cuts were pioneered, subgrade was groomed, finished, and ready for base rock;

I could envision every detail of the finished project laid out right in front of me.

At that time, I really didn't understand what I was seeing. I shook my head in disbelief, unsure of what was going on. *How can I see this in my mind when no one else can?* I like to call those moments "Weird-oh!"

The vision didn't do anything for me to get people on the right page on that project. It just put me on the cusp of a discovery. I had yet to implement the meaning of what I had learned from this moment. So, I was fighting with myself and trying to understand the crew members and why they couldn't see what I could!

> *I would get so damn frustrated with my team and myself that I wanted to run off and scream at the sky!*

One morning, I'd had it, and I stopped the D10 Dozer hand to change the haul road pattern he was carving out. I wanted him to cut in a new road for the scrapers that I was convinced would save cycle time seconds.

Let me explain . . . .

Cycle time refers to the time a scraper takes to make a round from the cut to the fill and back again. When I pointed out to the dozer hand what I thought was, in Lonnieism, "As obvious as a heart attack" or "a no-brainer," he stared at me like I was from another planet.

I shouted, "Josh, cut the friggin' road in right above that cleft in the hillside and bring it out over the draw by that low spot on the hill." He looked me square in the eye and said with a low growl, "What the hell are you looking at?" I had to get him off the Caterpillar (Cat) and walk him through the entire future haul road. Then, we walked back to his Cat in silence. He shot a flustered look my way and popped off, "How do you see that?" I yelled back, "It's clear as a bell, Josh. A blind man could see it." (Yes, I was a bit of a hothead back then. Glad I got over that!)

Josh still wasn't getting me, and my blood pressure went up another notch. I barked, "Just cut the road in, my brother from another mother, and let's speed up these effin' scrapers. Time is money!" We gave each other the thumbs-up sign, and off I went.

This same scenario played out many times over the following months. I kept wondering, *what am I doing wrong? Am I not communicating clearly? Ugh. How come I can't make clear what I am seeing?*

Then, one day, I was checking out a deep fill slope that one of our master dozer operators was putting the finishing touches on. This guy was what one of my great mentors, Herman Hall, would call a pro. I could hear him say, "He's a pro, Lonnie . . . . He's a natural born." Boy, was he ever! Jim was incredible on a dozer and could do things with a Cat D10 or Cat D9 that no one else could do.

As I scanned the slope he was working toward, I thought I saw a "bust" in the grade—meaning the slope ratio didn't look quite right. It was very subtle, but my eyes and brain instantly picked out the anomaly.

Now, Jim could do work with no grade stakes. He had a helluva eye for grades. It was almost eerie what he could see and do with that dozer. We all used to joke that he wasn't human because he could work miracles with that Cat. I walked down the slope to him and gave him the park sign (you might recognize it as a "time out" gesture given on the football field). He parked, stepped out on the track, and hollered, "Hey, Blondie, what ya need?" That's another nickname I picked up, but it's a different story for a different time.

I jumped up on the Cat, pointing at the grade on the slope, and said, "Big Jim, am I just seeing things, or is that a bust in the slope?"

He gave me his big ol' grin and simply said, "It sure as hell is. I saw it right off. You see it, too. Nobody else can see it on this spread. I will fix it when I get to it."

I stared back at him and asked, "Have you ever wondered how we can see this stuff and no one else can?"

He let out a big laugh and quietly responded, "Lonnie, I call it 'the gift.' It is your gift you have been given. Only you and I have it. You can't expect anyone else to see it because they don't have it."

"Wow, Big Jim, that is pretty heavy stuff," I said, shaking my head. "Are you gettin' all philosophical on me?" He laughed and said, "That's why you have such a hard time with the guys. You have to understand that *you* can see what *they* can't see. Simple as that. You have to clearly explain to them what you are seeing, so they can eventually see it. Remember, Morelock, there is only one you."

Then Jim jumped back in the seat of his Cat, gave me a wave, and put his dozer back in the dirt. I walked away, perplexed by his statement: "Remember, Morelock, there is only one you!"

What the hell did he mean by that?

As I climbed the slope and walked back to my truck, the entire conversation hit me like someone whacking me upside my head with a baseball bat. No wonder I always got so pissed off and frustrated. No wonder these guys didn't understand me. What Big Jim explained was an epiphany. I had a gift that many of my team didn't have, and I had to come to grips with that. How many Lonnie Morelocks are there? Easy answer. Only one! My mind swirled. This was just like being in high school with all my different teammates—recognizing their skills and mine.

There was only one of each of my teammates. They had gifts I didn't have. In fact, everyone has a gift no one else has. WHAT A CONCEPT!

I immediately realized I needed to change my tactics when explaining what I saw, what I wanted done, and what I was trying to achieve. Shortly after Jim jolted me with the truth, I started working on my new approach with the crew. The turnaround in them was magnificent. Their respect level for me went through the roof. I started learning what it meant to be a trainer right then and there. I was helping others see what they couldn't see, but what I could see was in Lonnieisms "as obvious as a heart attack!" *Way cool!*

IT JUST GOT CLEARER

As I continued in my career, I saw more qualities in people they could not see in themselves. I noted leadership talent and ability in people who did not believe they had these traits. I worked hard at perfecting how to bring those talents and abilities out of them, to help them improve and be all they could be. It was a satisfaction that could not be measured. I started to love the feel of it, and I wanted more!

My mind went back to another one of my great mentors, a master blade operator named Bob. I was his grade setter for over two years, and Bob took me under his wing and taught me the art of earthmoving and finish blade operations.

One day, late in the morning, Bob stopped his blade and yelled at me to jump up into the cab. He wanted to talk to me. I climbed up the ladder and stepped onto the deck of the blade. Bob gave me a gaze I had never seen before. Something in his eyes told me I was about to hear some profound wisdom.

Bob locked eyes with me and said, "Lonnie, all that you will accomplish in your career will mean nothing. Yes, you have an awesome future ahead of you. But what is really going to matter is the positive impact you will have on all those around you."

As I stared back at him, I briefly thought a tear came into his eye. He was staring right through me so hard that the hair on my arms stood up. A warm glow flowed through me. Bob took hold of my arm and whispered, "Never forget that." Then he gave me a pointed smile and said, "Now, get off my blade and get back to work."

Driving home that day, I thought a lot about what Bob said. I could never imagine where his prophetic "words of wisdom" would lead me someday.

With Jim's and Bob's new wisdom in mind, I worked through my career, mentoring and training new supervisors. When I started my business as a field supervisor trainer, I realized that one of my greatest attributes was helping people see that there is only one of them.

TURBO SMART

A grand example of applying these epiphanies to my trainings (and there are many) was when I had the pleasure of working with a vice president of operations. Shane was incredibly intelligent and a gifted estimator. He could put together Excel spreadsheets like no one I had ever seen. He was, as I liked to define brilliant individuals, turbo-smart!

During our training, when Shane began working with his direct reports, the project managers, and project engineers under him, he would get so angry and frustrated that they could not do what he could.

It seemed so simple to him. He would call me, all in a tither, and spout, "Why can't they just do what I ask them to do?"

I then had to give him the lesson I had learned long ago: "There Is Only 1 of You."

I replied slowly and calmly, "There is only one Shane."

As I had been with Big Jim, the dozer hand, Shane was puzzled. "Lonnie, what do you mean there is only one Shane?"

I proceeded to give him the full explanation. "Shane, there is only one of you. Only one. You have gifts and talents no one else has. You cannot expect your people to see what you see and do what you do because they are not you. You have to show them the way. You have to take every one of them and walk them through your distinct processes and procedures so they can thoroughly understand what you want from them. You have to teach and train them to see what you see. It takes a huge amount of patience, practice, and understanding, but when they 'get it,' and I mean truly 'get it,' you will be thrilled with the end result."

Shane's crinkled brow told me he was unsure he could pull this off, but I, again, stressed the importance of one-on-one interaction and extreme patience.

We put together a program and approach to help him do exactly that with his team. A phone call I received from him a few months later said it all. After winning a great bid, Shane was ecstatic and yelling through the phone. As introverted as Shane was, I had never heard him really get excited! I had never witnessed ecstatic emotion like this from him. It was exhilarating.

He hollered, "My guys really came through. They are all on their game. What a turnaround!"

I gently replied, "Shane, go look in the mirror. The face you see staring back at you is who did it! You are learning the lesson of 'There Is Only 1 of You,' and you are training your team to see what you see."

I continued, "Now, get ready for one hell of a ride going forward because your entire group is only going to continue to improve. Way to go! I am super proud of you, and you should be proud of your-self!"

> *There are not enough pages in this book to share all the ex-amples of teaching and witnessing the favorable results of the lesson, "There is Only 1 of You."*

I don't just mean the experiences I have had teaching it; I mean watching the men and women I have taught it to put it into action and how their professional lives and teammates' lives have changed because of it.

As a leader, you must be able to help your counterparts, your team members, and all the people you supervise to learn this very valuable leadership lesson.

Each one of us is a completely different person from anyone else, with different God-given gifts, talents, and abilities. No one has yours. They are yours and yours alone. Use them to help people see what you see.

Learn to make your vision perfectly clear.

Paint the picture.

Learn how to help people see and follow you in the direction you want them to go.

Then, help them share that concept with their peers.

This is by far one of a leader's greatest recipes for accomplishment.

The personal satisfaction of successfully achieving this is priceless.

RUN AT YOUR PROBLEMS

"Houston, we have a problem!" These are the iconic words of Jack Swigert, command module pilot of Apollo 13, uttered to let Mission Control know that something was very wrong with their command module.

WOW!

I've always marveled at what must have been going through his crew's minds when the oxygen tanks blew, and they were 200,000 miles away from Earth, on their way to the Moon. In deep space, with their ship crippled, they knew they were in big trouble. Talk about a major problem. A problem that developed into a friggin' nightmare. Three lives hung in the balance.

There was painful silence when NASA Mission Control in Houston first heard these words. A gut-wrenching dread fell over the entire ground control team. Everyone realized it was bad, but during that first call of distress, they didn't know the half of it. The awesome movie *Apollo 13*, starring Ed Harris, Tom Hanks, Kevin Bacon, Bill Paxton, and many other great actors, is another of my all-time favorite flicks. It demonstrates leadership training at its finest.

Both James Lovell and Gene Kranz, Director of Mission Control in Houston, were outstanding in their leadership roles. Gene never missed a beat. He was like the rock of Gibraltar. Failure never entered his mind. He had no concept of it or of running from the problem. He was focused! He was intense! He made his expectations crystal clear by issuing the order: "We've never lost an American in space; we're sure as hell not gonna lose one on my watch! Failure is not an option." Ed Harris', i.e., Gene Kranz's exact words to his team, are pretty clear to me. Crystal clear!

I have often wondered, had there been different leaders involved in Apollo 13, would the outcome have been different? Thankfully, we will never know because the leadership team's "Running at the Problem" saved the day, saved the mission, and saved the lives of three astronauts on that crippled spaceship. INCREDIBLE.

I still remember how I felt when I first watched this movie years ago. Chills swept through me as I marveled at the display of absolute leadership, problem-solving, and the tenacious approach to making what seemed like the impossible happen.

Damn, I might just have to stop writing and go watch Apollo 13 again. Okay, can't do that right now. Got to keep the thought process going.

THE DISAPPEARING LEADER

I had taken a job for a small earthmoving contractor early in my career. The project would result in a future high-security prison in far Northern California. In the beginning, the beauty of this job was that it was to be 7 days a week, 12 hours a day. The work window was short due to the location of the project and the NorCal rainy season starting early. Time was a factor, as 637 Scrapers do not function well in the mud!

I took the job wholeheartedly because, at this time in my young life, I wanted to buy my first house. I figured a few months of 7–12s, as they called it, in dirt movin' lingo, and I would make a jang (buttload) of money, and "Operation Buy a House" would proceed according to plan. *Sweet*!

When I first got to the project, the monumental amount of dirt moving it would take to mass grade the site was staggering. A great friend of mine, to this day, was going up to work on the same project. He was a top-notch scraper operator and was becoming an extremely competent grade setter. I had never met the grading foreman. When I did get the opportunity to meet him on my first day, my Spidey Sense immediately started tingling.

I shrugged it off and walked to my 637, fondly waiting for me in the equipment lineup. She was a thing of beauty. I climbed up the ladder, settled comfortably in the seat, and went to work.

The material was pure, bona fide "potato dirt"—the thrill of every scraper operator on the planet! It was easy loading and smooth dumping, perfect for making haul roads resembling the track at the Daytona 500 Speedway. I thought I'd entered a dirt-moving paradise and died and gone to heaven. The entire scraper crew and I were having a great time.

Unfortunately, we were to soon discover who we were working for. On the second day, a scraper got hopelessly stuck in some over-wet material similar to a mud bog.

The 637 was a behemoth mechanical dinosaur buried in quicksand, literally sinking in the mud.

As the other teams continued to work, passing the stuck machine time and time again, I wondered, *where is the foreman? Why isn't he dealing with this*!? The operator sat perplexed on the dirt bank next to his floundering machine. The look on his face said, *is nobody coming to help me?*

After what seemed like an eternity, here came Val, his grade-setting gear flying as he ran to the stuck scraper. He looked around with a red face, and I could read his thoughts: *what the f___? Why aren't we working to get this rig unstuck*!?" He darted off in the direction of the equipment lineup/maintenance yard area, and in what seemed like seconds, he showed up again, this time with the master mechanic, some heavy-duty chokers, and a D9 Dozer following closely behind.

They hooked up the choker to the D9; the master mechanic took care of the hand signals, and the 637 was easily pulled out of the quagmire. Val then developed a plan to excavate around the mud bog, using the D9 as support, until the wet material, i.e., the mud bog, was quickly taken care of.

The entire time all this was going down, the foreman was no-where to be seen. We never learned where he had gone. This same sort of scenario played out many times over the next few months. He was nowhere to be found whenever there was an issue of any kind. Then, matters spiraled downhill. Some days, the fog would set in, making visibility marginal. As soon as a problem developed in the cuts or fills, he disappeared.

Val always came to the rescue.

For obvious reasons, we nicknamed the foreman "The Invisible Man."

Whenever there was a problem, he just vanished. It was abso-lutely incredible—in the worst way. However, from watching Val in action, I learned the importance of "Running at a Problem." The entire crew had great respect for Val.

Understandably, they all whispered the same sentiment over and over: "Val should be running this show." After several more months, I got a job offer closer to home, so I gave my notice and moved on. I never met up with that foreman again. Thank God!

Val went on to become a very successful earthmover. That didn't surprise me a bit. Then he outdid himself and became that great foreman he should've been. Even better . . . he progressed to superintendent before finally quitting to launch his own earthmoving company, which he still successfully runs today. I knew he would go far!

I experienced many instances of "Disappearing Leader" syndrome as I grew in my career—too many to tell. What I learned is that any team leader, no matter the size or type of job they are overseeing, must always be the first to "Run at the Problem." They must be the first to attack it and immediately work with the team to develop a solution. *What Makes a Team Tick* is knowing, without a doubt, that every team member can always, 110%, depend on their leader to solve problems, have their back, and be there to help them when they most need it.

A leader is dependable, reliable, and trustworthy . . . when the chips are down, and, in textbook construction lingo, the shit is hitting the fan—I always wondered what that would actually look like. And now I know—a big mess for sure.

What truly makes a team tick is when every single member is an intense problem solver. They are all Jim Lovells and Gene Kranzs—a testament to the leadership training of Apollo 13.

MAJOR DAM

One of my most successful projects is a great testament to this concept. It was a major dam repair with difficult access challenges, material processing and placement issues, super strict tolerances, specifications, and on and on.

> *The job startup, out of the gate, was a rocky one!*

The project team and I thought we had a great plan. Unfortunately, each and every pre-thought-out plan for the work operations was going to "hell in a handbasket"—another well-known Lonnieism. Actually, I think I borrowed that one from my dad. Now that is funny!

In short, the project was struggling. The owner's representatives were getting that "Can these guys get this built?" look in their eyes. I was beginning to get, shall we say, slightly worried as the uneasiness in my gut grew exponentially.

Then, as I was driving home one night, I passed by a major Air Force base. An F-16 Fighter, probably in training, flew right over the top of me. I could feel the heat from the engine afterburners, and the noise was deafening. I blinked in disbelief, and as I watched that jet disappear into the wild, blue yonder, I immediately thought of Apollo 13.

I told myself, *Lonnie, you must become like Gene Kranz. You have an entire team of Jim Lovells. Use this to your advantage. You've got this*!

A wave of positivity, excitement, and enthusiasm enveloped me. I closed my eyes (just briefly, of course, because I was still driving my coveted company truck), and I clearly saw the "finished product picture" of the job in my mind. I could hear Gene Kranz's voice whispering in my ear, "Mission accomplished."

The next morning, early, before the start of the shift, I gathered the whole supervisor team together, staff and craft, and announced: "Team, we have a problem! This is the Apollo 13, and FAILURE IS NOT AN OPTION! Now, let's use the unlimited talent in this room and figure out every single problem. Are you with me?"

The roar was tremendous. The "Let's Make It Happen!" attitude rolled through the group like a tidal wave. We went on to brainstorm and attack every problem. One remarkable solution swiftly built upon the other. Out-of-the-box thinking was the rule of the day. Every field supervisor RAN at every problem. We got the equipment operators involved. We got the truck drivers involved. We got the laborers involved. We got the mechanics with their never-ending MacGyver abilities involved. We got the owner's reps involved.

The entire project team became a knock-off of NASA, Apollo 13, and Houston Mission Control. One problem after another was overcome, and the project turned around; enthusiasm, passion, and a winning spirit grew and grew. Morale went through the roof. The project was a huge success!

Moral of the Story: Every team member became a problem solver. No potential solution was looked down upon as a "stupid idea" or was not fully considered. What we had was a non-stop smorgasbord of ideas and innovation.

Every problem or issue was run at head-on until a viable solution was developed. The entire team was ticking—just like a Rolex watch!

You want to know "What Makes a Team Tick?" Running at Problems!

Running at Problems is a major key element to bolster the positive attitude needed in your problem-solving approach. Do not be a "Disappearing Leader." Be an immediate problem solver. Involve your team in everything.

Finally, don't forget these leadership concepts, which will always lead to Absolute Teamwork!

- Do Not Be a Disappearing Leader
- Run at Your Problems
- Prioritize the Problems
- Solve One Problem at a Time
- Reach out for Help—Immediately
- Get the Right People Involved
- Be Open to Every Single Idea for a Solution
- Focus on Absolute Teamwork in Problem-Solving

CHAPTER 3

KNOWING YOUR ROLE

"The key to teamwork is to learn a role, accept the role, and strive to become excellent playing it."
—Pat Riley

B efore anyone can become proficient in a role, they must know what their role is.

Before you, as a leader, can become a leader, you must Know Your Role.

What exactly are you supposed to be doing consistently day in and day out?

Do you know your responsibilities?

Are you in control of your immediate operations?

Are you where you are supposed to be when you are supposed to be there?

Or . . . are you a Disappearing Leader, as we talked about in the last chapter?

THE FIRST RUNG OF THE LADDER

When I became a grading foreman, I was nervous as hell. I was now in charge of all the mass grading operations I had been a part of as an equipment operator and grade setter. Truthfully, I was scared to death. Who was going to tell me exactly what I was supposed to be doing?

I will never forget the first day out.

I got the crew gathered up. Everyone huddled around, and all the "old timers," as we respectfully called them, watched me intently. Everyone shot me expressions like, *okay, Lonnie, let's get this show on the road.* I could hear negative whispers all around me. "Oh, look . . . Lonnie is the big man now." And sadly, "What a joke."

I focused really hard on not hurling my guts out. After a few deep breaths, I regained my composure, began the startup safety meeting, and briefly reviewed the day's operation . . . very briefly. I just wanted to get the hell out of the group and send the team on their way. At this point, I had no idea what it meant to be a leader. I had no clue what it meant to be the foreman. All I knew was that I was now in charge. After I dismissed the meeting, I walked off to my company truck and softly whispered to myself, "Help me, God."

It took all of two days for me to earn my first nickname. Running around the project with my hair on fire, screaming and yelling at the top of my lungs, spinning in circles like a rotating top . . . and I actually thought I was doing a good job. NOT!

At lunch break, one of the crewmembers, who never really liked me to begin with, yelled out in front of everyone, "Hey, here comes the Tasmanian Devil." That was it. That was my new nickname. I had now become my worst nightmare . . . the Tasmanian Devil, aka Taz! The second I heard that nickname, I was gut-shot and embarrassed. A dark shadow followed me around all day until quitting time.

I was reminded of the Tasmanian Devil on the old Bugs Bunny cartoons, spinning around all over the place like a tornado, destroying everything and never doing anything right.

I thought long and hard about how the day had gone as I drove home that night. Beat down, discouraged, and pissed off, I was ready to throw in the towel. Screw being a foreman. I don't need this shit!

My mind kept returning to my new nickname and what I'd thought about when I heard it. I remembered the old cartoons I'd watched as a kid. Bugs Bunny, the Road Runner, and Yosemite Sam were all solid characters. Then there was me—the idiot Tasmanian Devil. They weren't wrong. That whole day, I had spun around like a tornado from one location to another, leaving nothing but devastation in my path. *Ugh. Is that really who I am?* A picture of my dad, grandpa, and uncle swam to the surface of my mind. These men were all great construction supervisors. *How did they do it? What was their secret?*

I dreaded driving into work the next morning. I heard the crew's laughter as I walked up to start the meeting. "Yo, . . . Tasmanian Devil, how ya doin'?!" Then roaring laughter! I got through the meeting—barely—and headed for my truck.

One of my many great mentors, Gene, hollered at me as I passed him in the fill. He was a master grade setter long before lasers and GPS were ever thought of. I pulled over, and he looked me in the eye and sternly said, "Let's go for a ride."

My heart sank. *What did I do now?*

As we drove around the project, Gene didn't say a word for a few minutes. Silence filled the air as I stared out the window. He then turned to me and said, "Lonnie, do you know what your role is here now?" It took all I had in me not to let one tear roll out of my eye. I looked right back at him and said, "No, Gene, I have *no friggin' idea* what the hell I am supposed to be doing." He dryly replied, "Well, that is pretty obvious, kid." I thought my debut as a foreman was finished.

He then cleared his throat, took a deep breath, and in his distinct Southern drawl, started in, "Lonnie, you have a ton of God-given talent. You know the work. You are a 'natural-born' earthmover. You have gifts to see things in advance—what no one else can see. You're smart, likable, and you treat your people great. But you are just running around like a chicken with your head cut off. Slow your ass down and RUN THE WORK. Know Your Role."

I turned to Gene and argued, "But that's it, Gene, I don't really know what my role is."

He continued, "First off, your role is safety. That is and always will be number one. Never forget that. The safety of all these hands is now your direct responsibility. Next, plan out each day. You know the work. You know what to do, and you know how to build it. Share your plan, thoughts, and ideas with the team every morning. Let them know what you are thinking. Study the plans and keep the grade setters dialed. Check in with them throughout the day and make sure they are doing everything correctly. Meet with the surveyors in advance and share any important information you got from them with the grade setters. Get yourself in a rhythm for the shift. Get in a cycle. Get on a working schedule with the different crews. Check in on fill. Spend a few minutes there, then go check in on the cut. Drive the haul roads and stay on top of the access to all locations on the job. Make sure everything is running smoothly. Don't spend too much time in one location. Make sure the operators are dialed, then move on. You are the leader now. You are not the grade setter; you don't do their job anymore. Let them do their job. You are not the blade hand or the dozer hand anymore. You are their leader. You are not the scraper operator. These guys are all pros. Let them do their jobs. You are the coordinator, the organizer, the set of eyes looking out in front, clearing away the potential obstacles or problems, and seeing the changes that will need to be made in advance. You are gifted at seeing these. Use those talents and abilities, and let your team do their jobs. Take care of them. Get them what they need to perform at the top of their game. When things go wrong, jump in, and solve the problem. Don't start yelling and screaming and getting all excited. What good does that do? Nothing except getting everyone all stirred up. Your role is to keep everything running smoothly. Going 200 miles per hour is not the answer. Smooth and controlled is the answer. Smooth and coordinated is the answer. Smooth and organized is the answer. Remember, 'young man,' slow is smooth, but smooth is fast. Take care of your team in every way you can. You are the symphony conductor, and they are playing all the instruments. Make music with them! You can do this. This is your destiny. You will go places you can't even imagine right now, but first, you must Know Your Role as a foreman and perform that role to the absolute best of your ability. Now take me back to fill before the blade hand gets ahead of himself!"

Gene went to step out of the truck, then turned to me one last time with a big ol' grin' on his face. He clearly stated, southern drawl and all . . . "Know Your Role."

I drove off thinking of the last couple of days. I thought of everything I hadn't been doing and what I should have been doing. That was it. I immediately pulled over off the haul road and made a detailed list of all the directions Gene had given me. I doubled down on all the areas I needed to focus on in my new role:

- Be prepared for and have a plan for the startup meeting.
- Have a plan for the entire shift.
- Check on the fill.
- Check on the cut.

- Check on the surveyors.
- Check on the grade setters.
- Schedule the crews in each location on the job, and stay on top of the schedule.
- Stay on top of the quantities for the shift.
- Look out in front of the crews.
- Solve potential problems before they can happen.
- Take care of the team and what they need to succeed.
- Be organized and coordinated at all times.
- Thoroughly understand the plans, so I can share my thoughts with the crews and get their input and ideas.
- Study the operations, and look at every way to improve them.
- Check on the mechanics and status of ongoing equipment repairs.
- And on and on and on . . .

Most important of all:

- Let my team do the work.
- Do not keep trying to do their jobs for them.
- Support them to be the best they can be.
- **BE THE LEADER.**

One week later, and after implementing the lessons from Gene, I was truly amazed at the difference in the project. I could *feel* the change. And I liked what I was feeling. There was a noticeable shift in the team's atmosphere. Their overall attitude was positive; they were motivated by the project's forward momentum. I could sense a new measure of respect and admiration from them. Nobody said anything, but I could feel it. I could see it in their eyes. My heart was on fire.

I knew I was home. I knew this was where I belonged.

At the end of the shift that next Friday, my old adversary walked up to me as I went to my truck. He looked me in the eye and said, "Ya know, Morelock, you're doin' a pretty damn good job. Guess I am going to have to promote you to 'Taz.'" I gave him a small smile and asked, "What the hell is Taz?" He smiled back, shook my hand, and said, "That is the Tasmanian Devil, in complete control."

I turned and walked away then, hiding the tear running down my cheek. I was on my way, and now I KNEW MY ROLE.

HOW TO KNOW YOUR ROLE

As a leader, it is imperative that you know every single part of your role. You must strive to perform your distinct role to the best of your ability. As a member of any team, Knowing Your Role is just as important. When every team member knows their specific role, then strives to, and eventually performs that role to the best of their ability . . . the overall effect is damn close to perfection.

That is when the magic happens. That is when Performance Above & Beyond is achieved. The end result is Absolute Teamwork.

Here's another example of the importance of **Knowing Your Role.**

I will call the person in this next anecdote Paul. When I first started running fieldwork as a civil grading foreman, a young grade setter, Paul, came to work for me. I knew nothing about this kid but that he was a go-getter. He worked his everlasting ass off. I used to think he was a direct relative of the Energizer Bunny. He never ran out of power but could run with a grading crew all day long, in 100-plus degrees in the hot California summer—all while never missing a beat. His work ethic was incredible.

The flip side of having such a newbie work for me was that he had a lot to learn about grade setting. One early morning, shortly after his first month, he caught me in my office. He strode confidently in the door and proclaimed, "Lonnie, I am ready to be a foreman."

I about fell out of my chair but answered him with a broad smile, "Really, Paul, and what makes you think you are ready to be a full-fledged foreman?" He answered back with no hesitation. "Lonnie, I know I can work hard, and I want to further my career in the construction industry. I am going to be a kick-ass supervisor." I couldn't help but admire his ambition and confidence, all rolled up into one determined package.

I directed, "Paul, take a seat. Let's talk about this." Once he sat, I gathered my thoughts and continued, "There is no doubt you are a bust-ass worker. You have an insatiable appetite to learn and improve. You want the operations to always run smoothly and be successful. You take a lot of pride in the quality of your work. But do you truly Know Your Role as a grade setter?"

Paul's eyebrows went up, so I knew he was listening.

"Paul, do you truly believe you have all the knowledge and ability to manage a full-on mass grading spread as a grade setter? You completely understand how to read plans—I mean every single aspect, the general note, typical details, and on and on—and know all that you are looking at when reviewing the grading plans?" Paul's confidence drooped a little, and so did his shoulders.

I wasn't done: "Now, honestly, ask yourself, do you know 110% of everything I just explained?" Paul shrugged. He was silent. I could feel the dejection flowing out of him.

At first, I panicked seeing this (without him knowing, of course) and thought, *oh no, I just completely deflated this young, upcoming superstar.*

42

I quickly regained my composure and said, "Paul, look at me. You are, without a doubt, an awesome grade setter. I wish half the crew had the grit, tenacity, and desire to continuously improve the way you have. Are you hearing me?"

When Paul lifted his head, I saw the gleam had returned to his eyes. *Whew.*

"Paul, you have all the inner drive, talent, and ability to be an absolutely outstanding civil grading foreman. You only lack one key ingredient: knowledge. Simple as that."

Then I proposed this question to him, "Do you completely understand your role as a grade setter? Do you completely understand all that is required of you in performing this role?"

That dejected look was creeping back onto his face. He quietly answered, "No, I guess I don't." I turned the tide of the conversation. "Okay, then, how do you think you would succeed as a foreman? If I were to promote you today, and you went out tomorrow and started supervising the entire crew, how would you know what that role entails? You wouldn't. So, I would be setting you up to fail. I won't do that."

Paul nodded, but now, he wasn't discouraged. He was thinking.

"You are too valuable of an employee, and your future is way too bright for me to set you up to fail. So, how 'bout this . . . . Let's work together going forward, and you can work with the foreman, too. Together, we will help you to completely understand your role as a grade setter. I will personally help you learn to read plans better. The foreman will be sure he is training you on all aspects of grade setting; I mean everything. How to set slope stakes accurately. How to calculate quantities. How to understand slope ratios and grade percentages and how to calculate them. How to set up subgrade layouts, finish pad layouts, front yards cut-offs, street gut sections, and everything else you need to know to nail down your role as a grade setter. We will develop a list together to keep you on track. When you learn everything there is to know about your role and can perform that role day in and day out, accurately and confidently, then we will discuss your future as a civil grading foreman. How does that sound?"

Paul's eyes lit up like a Christmas tree. He jumped out of his chair and said, "Lonnie, I am going to know my role as a grade setter better than any grade setter on this crew. I am going to be the best damn grade setter in the company. Now let's get started."

I stood up, shook his hand, and knew with my whole heart and soul this kid is going places.

Paul went on to work his heart out for the next six months. He learned his role and did exactly what he said he would do. He performed his grade-setting role like an Olympic champion. His knowledge and ability grew like a fertilized weed. His talent continued to improve, as did his skills and overall knowledge of his role. The following spring, the company picked up a tremendous amount of civil grading work, and we needed another competent civil grading foreman. I knew just the man for the job.

I will never forget calling Paul into my office after the first week of the startup of the new project. He sat down and asked me, "What's up?"

I drilled him dead in the eyes and said, "Do you now Know Your Role as a grade setter?" He stared back at me with that confident look and smiled. "Hell yes, Lonnie. I can truly say I believe I know my role. I still have more to learn, but I have a pretty damned good idea of what I am doing now and what is expected of me. Why do you ask?"

I didn't miss a beat.

"Paul, you have definitely proven yourself. You have learned well. So, now I would like to give you the opportunity to learn a new role. You are, starting right now, promoted to civil grading foreman. Congratulations!"

I thought he was going to jump through the ceiling of my office. He was hootin' and hollerin' so hard. He immediately sat down and said, "How do I know my role for this new role?" I burst with pride when he asked that question.

With a grin breaking through my face, I stated, "Paul, here is a binder I have developed from my past experiences as a grading foreman, with an entire breakdown of all your new responsibilities. This shows you, in detail, your new role. You have a lot to learn. The team will be by your side, teaching you and training you every step of the way."

I paused to let him take it all in. "Paul, you will not learn all of this overnight. It will take time and a lot of dedication. But I assure you, as you learn to Know Your Role and become super proficient at it, you will set yourself up for the next stage of your career. So, what are you going to do?"

He shook my hand wildly and exclaimed as I bit back a chuckle (and a few tears), "I am going to learn and know my role and be the best civil grading foreman ever!" Paul strode out of my office, and I wondered if his feet ever touched the ground. He was ready and willing to confront what lay ahead.

Paul went on to not only become a superstar grading foreman, he was promoted to field superintendent, project superintendent, and then general superintendent He learned the importance of Knowing Your Role and, most importantly, what it took to make that happen.

Throughout my career, I continued to learn the importance of Knowing Your Role and the significant value of every team member knowing their specific position.

I witnessed, over and over again, the monumental success of teams of builders who knew their distinct roles and positions and performed those roles to the best of their abilities.

As a leader, Knowing Your Role is the key to success.

Ensuring your team knows their role and giving them all the support you can to help them perform their roles takes that team to incredible performance levels. It opens the door to advancement for individuals desiring that direction in their careers. It builds the utmost confidence and trust in all the players so they can depend on each other no matter what they are up against on a project or what they are trying to achieve.

Know Your Role, and then enjoy the ride!

CHAPTER 4

WHAT ARE YOUR EXPECTATIONS?

"High expectations are the key to everything."
—Sam Walton

Expectations. It's a big word. Descriptive. Influential. Powerful. In fact, it's a colossal word.

It's also extremely descriptive to whoever you are sharing your expectations with. Expectations greatly influence a person's understanding of what you want and what you are trying to achieve. When they are communicated the right way, expectations are absolutely powerful. If you do not share your expectations with your team, how can you ever expect them to live up to what you want them to achieve??

When your team knows your expectations, it's a powerful force that gives them clues to eventually grasp the full understanding of the direction you want them to go.

*Expectations are the front doorstep, leading to open the door
that holds the knowledge of "What Makes Your Team Tick."*

The thought process is relatively simple. If my team does not know what I expect of them, how can I ever hope they will rise to the performance level I expect?

As I have noted, the other side is that I need to know what my team expects of me. If I do not know what my team expects of me, how will I know how to lead them?

How will I ever stand a chance of figuring out What Makes My Team Tick?

Let's take it one step further. If each team member does not know what the other team members expect of them, then how can they perform for their team at their highest optimum level?

DIRTY PLANS

Let me revert to my dirt-moving days as a foreman to give you a more in-depth example.

My team expected me to be planned out, coordinated, and organized. They expected me to know the plans and what we were building and, thusly, (another Lonnieism), be able to guide them through each day on the project.

In turn, I expected the haul road blade to keep the scraper haul roads as smooth as a new 5-lane freeway! I expected the dozer operators managing the cut to keep the ground ripped and processed in front of the scrapers so they could load more easily. I expected the fill Cat and compactors to keep up with the scrapers placing material, bringing up the fill slopes correctly, and keeping the fill smooth.

I expected the water truck drivers to apply the correct amount of water to the haul roads to maintain dust control and to keep the fills wet at the right moisture levels required for compaction. Most importantly, I expected the grade setters to maintain grade control on the entire project to ensure we were building the job right and per plan.

The team members had a plethora of continuous, identical expectations across the board. The scraper operators expected the haul road blade to keep the haul roads smooth, so they could, yes . . . haul ass! The scraper operators expected the water truck drivers to keep the haul roads wet to control dust but not so wet that they would lose traction and slide sideways, losing momentary control and, sometimes, in these moments of fear, filling their pants at the same time! The dozer operators expected the scraper operators to dump their loads correctly in the fill, maintain coordination with lift placements, and build the fill slopes correctly so the dozer operators didn't have to continuously keep pushing the slopes out. (Yes, this is civil grading jargon, but hopefully, you get my point). If the scraper operators did their jobs correctly, it took a lot of pressure off the dozer hands to fix issues "on the fly."

The scraper operators expected the dozer operators to keep the cuts ripped, processed, and fairly smooth to ease their loading process and not beat themselves to death bouncing over nuisance berms and large rocks while *not* ripping the ground deep enough, which would cause them to struggle to get a load.

It's a bit of a run-on explanation, but the gist is when all the operators were meeting not only my expectations but the expectations of each other, THE TEAM WAS TICKING!

The entire earthmoving team was clicking like a Rolex watch. They were dancing. Every member was meeting every other member's expectations. The overall result of the team's consistent performance was, without a doubt, Performance Above & Beyond. This outcome led daily to Absolute Teamwork. It was beautiful to behold and remarkable to be a part of.

On the flip side, when expectations were not met, total chaos and dysfunction ensued.

But we did not allow this to happen.

Why?

Because our expectations were made "crystal clear" daily, we expected each other to meet them consistently. There was never any doubt or gray area about what was anticipated.

We all worked our ever-lovin' hearts out to meet each other's expectations and took pride in this. We all wanted to perform at our optimum levels because we knew our team members depended on us to meet our expectations every day.

Again, and one more time for emphasis, we had to know what each team member expected so we could perform to the best of our ability. Additionally, everyone on the team knew we all were striving to constantly exceed expectations.

The camaraderie, pride, exhilaration of peak performance, and overall fun of the thrill of engagement kept us going and motivated. Knowing this drove us to achieve incredible results time and time again. It was a "Difference-Maker!"

As I continued to grow in my career and train field supervisors to be the best they could be, I concentrated not only on making my expectations comprehensive but also on making sure the field supervisors were developing and implementing their expectations of themselves and their crews.

I trained myself and them to expect safety as their number one priority, to expect the highest quality of work achievable, and to use absolute integrity in all their actions and decisions. We both knew to expect professional conduct from ourselves and every member of the team. We expected NO negative attitudes and for every member of the team to be treated with the highest levels of dignity, honor, and respect. No one ever expected to hear, "Can't." (Oh, using that word is a pet peeve of mine. There is no such thing as can't!)

No matter what role you play on your team, expect to give your absolute best every single day. Most importantly, adhere and live up to your expectations of yourself.

This list is repetitive. But it's powerful.

I'M A WHAT?

When I first became a general superintendent, as always, per my "mode of opperendus" (Lonnieism), stepping into a new role and a higher level of leadership and authority, made me as nervous as "a sick whore in church" as my dad would always say.

You would think that by this point in my career, I would have built up a pretty good chunk of self-assurance and have a high degree of self-confidence.

That wasn't the case at all!

I had a bad habit of second-guessing myself and letting that little sensation of "feeling unsure" creep in. Usually, I did not allow it to last very long, but it was always there, biting at my subconscious.

It was like a pesky mosquito hovering around my face that I kept swatting at to no avail. Being a superintendent overseeing a few key foremen and one major operation was demanding. Now, I was overseeing several superintendents and key foremen and supervising a number of different types of disciplines and crews.

My new project manager was little help. I had no guidance and was getting frustrated. Things were not going well. I knew I was struggling, but I couldn't quite put my finger on how to fix it.

Finally, after a few weeks of repeated trips to the project manager's office to hear how the job was in complete turmoil, I'd had my fill. The Lonnie of old (who I tried to suppress daily) came bubbling up, and I gave my project manager a taste of it. I strode angrily into his office and let loose, "I have no clue how to wrap my arms around all these different operations. You have never helped me to understand exactly what I am supposed to be doing and how I am supposed to do it. What the hell do you expect of me?!"

There was a long pause. I figured I would soon get what I like to refer to as "an opportunity to excel with another employer!" The project manager stared at me for an eternity until I wanted to find a hole to crawl in and hide. He then lowered his gaze, beckoned to the chair across from his desk, and calmly said, "Lonnie, take a seat."

I was 100% prepared for what I thought was coming. "Lonnie, you're fired."

Then he proceeded to blow my mind!

"Lonnie, you are absolutely correct," he calmly replied. "Thank you for opening my eyes to my failure of not taking the time to share my expectations of you with you. I assumed you would jump in and perform as your usual self. Taking charge, kicking ass, and taking names! My bad! Let's talk through this and get on the same page! As we all know, assumptions are the mother of all f___ups! I should have known better. I have been so wrapped up in my own world that I didn't take the time to see what was going on around me. How can you go be you in the new situation you are in if you don't know what you are supposed to be doing?"

John sighed, bowed his head, and continued before locking eyes on me again.

"So, how 'bout we sit right here and go through your new job description and decipher exactly what the roles, responsibilities, and, above all, the *expectations* are for being a general superintendent on this project? Sound good?"

I just about fell out of my chair. *Am I hearing right, or did I quietly step into the Twilight Zone, and Rod Serling is now talking to me, telling me his scary byline, "Welcome, Lonnie. You have now entered the Twilight Zone."*

If you're a younger reader with no idea what I am talking about, the *Twilight Zone* was a freaky-scary show in the late '60s that we used to watch as kids. It scared the living hell out of us most of the time. I thought for sure this was one of those times!

I regained my composure and responded in the calmest, most professional, authoritative voice I could muster. "Well, yes, John, let's do just that. I know I can knock this job out of the park. I know we have an awesome team. I just need to know how to step up and get my management skills to this next level of supervision quickly!"

We then sat there for well over an hour, and John went through, line by line, his expectations for me and the team, and he let nothing fall through the cracks! I was taking notes and writing like the speed of the wind in a Level 5 hurricane. I couldn't believe all he came up with and the depth of knowledge he displayed in that short 60 minutes. It was damn near overwhelming.

When he finished, and my arm and hand were about to fall off, he softly asked me, "Did you get all that? Did I help you understand my expectations and the new skills and abilities you need to learn to succeed? Have I set you up to succeed?"

I was flabbergasted!

He had gone from not giving me the time of day to giving me a full-on thesis for succeeding and achieving in my new role. Above all, his expectations were "crystal clear!" I was thrilled. I could feel the adrenaline pumping in my veins. I could feel the rush of excitement to get out to the project and put into practice the litany of advice and knowledge he had shared with me. Right then and there, I knew, without the slightest doubt, that I was on my way to taking my career to the next level. Now, I was *on fire!*

I returned to Earth and composed myself once more, trying hard not to let him see the newly regenerated "eye of the tiger" in me. I almost started humming the *Rocky* theme song.

I looked John squarely in the eye and said, "John, thank you so much for sharing all of this with me. I clearly see my mission now; I have a lot to learn and a lot to do. But I will assure you of this! With this most valuable information you have just given me, going forward, I will succeed; this team will succeed; this project will friggin' succeed, and I will make damn sure that you succeed."

John let out a big hearty laugh and boomed, "Go, get 'em, Wolfpack!" That pushed me over the edge.

As I walked out of his office, I swore I heard my grandpa's voice in my head, "Always remember, son, a rising tide floats all boats." As I jumped in my company truck and drove out onto the project, feeling a new wave of confidence washing over me that bright, sunny afternoon and squinting through the sun's glare on the windshield, I could clearly see the tide coming in!

When you share your expectations with your team, when a leader shares their expectations with another leader, and when the team shares their expectations of each other with each other, magic happens.

What were once considered "plateaus of performance" are obliterated. Overall achievement levels become like the *Star Trek* moniker. They are ". . . going places where no man has gone before."

Teamwork, morale, camaraderie, respect, pride, and admiration take on new meanings among team members who share their expectations and accomplishments.

> *Be diligent in sharing your expectations. Don't hold them inside. Share them. Really share them. With all your heart, share them.*

THEN SIT BACK AND WATCH YOUR TEAM TICK!

CHAPTER 5

KNOW YOUR PEOPLE— WHAT MAKES THEM . . . THEM?

"If your team is not performing well, take a peek in the mirror."
—Ken Blanchard

I have always loved this quote, especially when trying to analyze what is wrong with the team I am leading. It is a real eye-opener when you look in the mirror and realize that you are directly responsible for your team's lack of performance. In my experience, I can tell you that the main reason stems from not really knowing your people working for you.

When you do not truly know your people and their distinct skills, talents, and abilities, you have no way of knowing where to put them on the team to set them up to succeed. Your inability to do this keeps you from leading your team to the performance levels you are trying to achieve.

The serious questions you have to ask yourself are as follows:

Who is on your team?

I mean, who are they, really?

Do you even know?

Most importantly, do you *want to know?*

The direct, unequivocal answer to all those questions is a resounding YES!

Here is the next question.

If you do not know your people and have no idea of what makes them them, then how will you ever know "What Makes Your Team Tick?" You can't, and you won't, so, theoretically, you will NEVER achieve all you want or wish for with your team. YOU HAVE TO KNOW THEM!

I do not mean you have to know *everything* about them. You don't have to know and be involved with their personal life. You certainly do not have to be their friend. I mean, what makes each one of them tick? This is the ultimate answer we are looking for, which you, as a leader, should be looking for, too.

KNOW WHAT MAKES A PERSON UNIQUE

Personalities are always a bit of a struggle for a leader. Why is that?

This answer is easy.

If you're an overachiever, you may have already figured out this answer. The "why" is that each of us has our own distinct, God-given personality and characteristics. We are all unique. One of a kind. No one else is like us.

Remember how we talked about "*There Is Only 1 of You*" in Chapter 2?

Our bestowed special talents, skills, and abilities are ours. We, and we alone, possess them. They are nobody else's. Again, as stated previously, they are _unique and_ exclusive to everyone. Let's pause here for one minute and reach for the ol' *Webster's Dictionary*. It states that the definition of unique is: "Being the only one; being without like or equal; distinctively characteristic. Sole, unequaled, peculiar."[4]

WOW! Now, that is some heavy stuff. I know, for a fact, that I, Lonnie Morelock, am a sole individual. There is no one like me. I am unequaled. Yes, for damn sure, I am peculiar. But that is the message I am trying to get across here.

I am ME.

You are YOU.

They are THEM.

The sheer beauty of this concept is that when you put yourself and all of THEM together, and you utilize everyone's unique talents and abilities, "bringing to bear" the very best of each individual's capabilities, you have a powerhouse team that can make shit happen!

You have a team that can go places and accomplish the unbelievable. I'm talking about achievements you think are way out of the realm that even you, as the leader, may not have thought possible. I am talking about achieving the impossible! What no team has ever done before!

---

4   "Unique Definition & Meaning." Merriam-Webster. Accessed November 17, 2024. https://www.merriam-webster.com/dictionary/unique.

This is why it is so vitally essential for you to know your people. This explanation, which we will investigate in much more detail, is monumental. It is staggering. It is astonishing. It is awe-inspiring. ABOVE ALL, I like to call it the "Difference-Maker." To learn "What Makes Your Team Tick" is to learn how to lead them in the direction you want them to go.

When you 100% know your team members' personalities, talents, and distinct abilities, you can put them in positions to succeed. You can put them in positions that work perfectly in their supporting role within the team. Each of them then puts their talents and abilities, which no other team member has, to the forefront of helping the team be the best they can be. And when you get all these individual talents, abilities, and personalities working together, continuously improving, and supporting each other, clicking like a Rolex watch, that is when the freakin' magic happens. That is when Performance Above & Beyond is engaged, and Absolute Teamwork is achieved. Next in line is colossal success! Realizing the Impossible follows close behind.

Now, the above never means that everyone goes together like peanut butter and jelly. Or warm peach cobbler and vanilla ice cream. Oh, yes, an all-time favorite of mine. Or buttery mashed potatoes and brown gravy. Another all-time favorite. Damn, my mouth started watering just thinking about it.

Anyway . . .

> *Your people and their personalities may not go together at all. They may be like oil and water—completely on the other side of the spectrum in compatibility.*

But . . . when you pair them with their specific, outstanding talents and abilities, that is a whole other story.

60

WE COME TOGETHER 'CAUSE OPPOSITES ATTRACT

One of my most successful mass grading teams was made up of a myriad of personalities and characteristics that did not complement each other in any way. Like in NO WAY. Everyone was absolute opposites.

Travis was Mr. Positive. He wore "rose-colored glasses." To him, every day was a beautiful day.

Dean was Mr. Negative. His nickname was Eeyore, after the gray donkey from *Winnie the Pooh*. "Oh no. Uh-oh, things are looking terrible. It's really bad . . . . What are we gonna do?"

Jeff was the "Little Red Hen"—who was more like a banty rooster—strutting around and screaming expletives all day long.

Chad was Mr. Serious. He was super-controlled, analytical, and always to the point.

Brent was Mr. Softy, aka "the reserved one." He was very quiet. "I want to make no waves and just do my job."

Kirk was the loudmouth who never had anything good to say.

Bill was the immoral degenerate. Filth just flowed from his entire being.

Katie was Ms. Happy Go Lucky, a free spirit. Wherever she went, she sang songs of happiness all day long.

Sue was the Lieutenant Commander. All she said was, "Get it done" and "Hurry up!" AND ON AND ON.

As you can see, each team member had their own memorable characteristics but those had nothing to do with their talents and how everyone orchestrated together.

Travis was a superstar earthmover.

Dean was a superstar master finish foreman and finish blade hand.

Jeff was an awesome grade setter and laid out grade stakes like Secretariat running to win all the races of the Triple Crown.

Chad was all business. He was super brilliant, an amazing engineer, and a superb problem solver.

Bill was a master dozer operator and a master finish dozer hand.

Kirk was a master excavation dozer hand and could support a scraper fleet like an aircraft carrier team supports the fighter pilots.

Brent was beyond analytical and outstanding with spreadsheets, specifications, and plan reviews. He helped the team know exactly what they needed concerning building the work.

Katie was another highly talented grade setter who knew finish layout like no other.

Sue was a pure, detail-focused taskmaster—and, in my eyes, a brilliant engineer and future supervisor. AND SO MUCH MORE.

When I put these people in their respective roles so they could support the team and each other with their talents, skills, and abilities, the combination was a Game-Changer. This team, and many more members of this team, people whom I do not have enough space or time to mention, went on to achieve super-human performances on one major civil project after another.

They were definitely warm peach cobbler and vanilla ice cream.

Despite making magic on the site, they all did not get along. I seriously could not stomach some of them, and many of them could not stomach each other. I more than loved and adored some of them. A few of them loved, admired, and adored a few more.

It was a vicious circle. But, because they all greatly respected each other's talents, skills, and abilities, and this respect level was shared and fostered amongst themselves, they gave their entire all for the team. Day in and day out! They were there for the top-notch performance and overall success of the team. Nothing else mattered.

There are not enough words in *Webster's Dictionary* to describe the experience of being a part of a superstar-winning team like this. And there are not enough positive adjectives to list. It is a boundless, limitless level of complete satisfaction breeding unadulterated high performance and tremendous success.

Knowing your people and all they can do and how they can do it for the betterment of the team gives you the required knowledge to set them up to succeed, which then sets your team up to succeed.

You also get the opportunity to help individuals grow in their respective careers and become all they are destined to be. Knowing your people allows you to open doors for them to better know themselves and push themselves to limits they never thought they could achieve. It all starts with genuinely taking the time and effort to know and understand them and to develop ways to help them continuously improve. The feeling of satisfaction and accomplishment that you get from helping a person in such a way is nearly unfathomable and becomes the groundwork for building and developing people. Give it a try! Get to know your team, then get them what they need to succeed.

THE NEXT TIME YOU LOOK IN THE MIRROR, YOU WILL LOVE WHAT YOU SEE.

CHAPTER 6

LET'S TALK—THE ART OF EFFECTIVE COMMUNICATION

"Communication is the key to teamwork and success. When we fail to communicate, failure always follows close behind."
—Lonnie S. Morelock, 2008

COMMUNICATION. Wow. It is truly becoming a lost art these days. With all the social media, emails, and texts, it feels like no one wants to talk with anyone anymore. Actual verbal communication is almost unheard of.

"Get with the times," everyone says. "Just send me a text or shoot me an email." "I will respond when I get a chance." Not to mention the lack of emotion or getting to the true meaning of what you are explaining, everything just goes out the window.

Now, I get that modern technology is a great thing.

But . . . there is still a lot to be said for real communication and its importance as an ingredient in any leader's and team's success. In all my experiences, good communication is a Game-Changer. It promotes confidence, teamwork, and camaraderie. Flat out, it brings success.

The absence of good communication can bring the exact opposite, resulting in a lack of knowledge, understanding, and absolute failure. Poor communication leads to an individual or team being unsure of themselves. They do not know what is expected of them and/or what you want them to achieve.

Communication breakdowns on the job site can be catastrophic, both from a building and application standpoint and as they relate to serious safety or quality issues.

Communication drives the bus. Without it, you have no idea where you are going or how you will get there.

Following a major problem that caused real issues on a project I was managing, I coined this quote that drives home everything I just related in the sentences above: "Communication is the key to teamwork and success. When we fail to communicate, failure will always follow close behind." That is the dead-nuts truth!

THE MOST MEMORABLE SPEECHES

When I think of examples of beautiful, articulate, passionate, and, above all, effective communication, I look back at my love for history. The first thing that comes to mind is Abraham Lincoln's "Gettysburg Address." The Battle of Gettysburg, the ravages of the Civil War, the country pitted against itself, and the thousands and thousands of soldiers who lost their lives. No matter what side of the battle you were on or your differences or beliefs, Abraham Lincoln brought everyone together, touching hearts, minds, and souls.

The "Gettysburg Address" has gone down in history as one of the greatest speeches of all time.

Martin Luther King Jr.'s famous "I Have a Dream" speech demonstrates unprecedented power in communication. To this day, his speech is still revered as the greatest civil rights speech of all time. The hearts and souls he touched, and the minds changed with his beliefs, thoughts, and feelings concerning the importance of civil rights and equality for all people changed the course of history, and rightfully so.

I can think of multiple talks and speeches I have heard at conventions, corporate business meetings, and on projects, and I know how powerful superior communication is. Chills would roll through me when I heard content transcending my soul. It leaves me in awe for a while. When this happens, you know you have been truly *moved*.

It is not only the essence of the communication that leaves us in awe; it is the intense feeling of the communication that causes that feeling.

Many times, we are rocked so completely that we never forget what we've heard for the rest of our lives. That is the beauty of effective communication.

When leaders talk to their team and can express themselves with incredible emotion, the team absorbs the information much more efficiently. They will be so much more receptive to what is being shared or taught as they become totally and completely engaged—their minds become one with the leader! When that happens, look out. That team is about to go out and make the impossible happen!

An influential and passionate speech can change the trajectory of lives. You can train, teach, and mentor at a higher level by utilizing good and effective communication. No matter if you're articulating work that needs to be done, changes to operations, issues, or problems, or directing a dysfunctional team trying to get back on track, the more effective and beautiful the communication, the more positive the outcome.

PUT YOURSELVES IN THEIR HEARTS AND MINDS

When you are communicating to people who you want to hang on your every word, they have to be able to feel what you are feeling. You can't just talk at somebody. You have to talk to them. Whether it is a direct report, a supervisor, a colleague, a team member, or hell, if you're talking to your wife or kids, it does not matter; talk to them.

When communicating with people, you do not just communicate with them. You "feel" to them, and you want them to "feel" you.

Now, I know you're thinking, *Lonnie, what the hell are you talking about? Have you gone off your rocker?*

What I am talking about is the way you communicate what you're feeling. Infusing passion into your speech is so much more powerful than just talking. You're not just talking to your team. And if your team is the one doing the talking, utilizing what you have taught them, they are not just talking to each other.

They are feeling you, and/or they are feeling each other. They are picking up what you are throwing down inside their bodies, souls, and minds.

That is *feeling* communication, not just talking communication. It is communicating on another dimensional level. And it is powerful!

Let's say you are trying to make a valid point to your team to improve an operation on your project. Your tone, facial expressions, and arm and hand gestures all come together to express what you feel in your heart and mind. You are speaking your point in a way so that they feel and truly understand what is being communicated to them. You are explaining the "why" without telling them the "why." You are involving them in your thought process, making them feel they are an important part of the solution.

To be an effective communicator, your listener must feel what you are feeling. You can talk AT THEM all day long, but it won't move them much.

Here are some examples:

"I want you to do this."

"I want you to do that."

"Take care of this."

"Take care of that."

"How come you are not doing this?"

"How come you are not doing that?"

THAT is talking "AT" them, and, in my opinion, it is disrespectful.

It IS NOT talking "TO" them.

When you talk to them, you communicate what you are feeling. Strive for your audience to pick that up. You want that *feeling* you are communicating to sink into their psyche.

KEEP IMPROVING

I used to talk so excitedly that I rushed my speeches along at 200 MPH. And, as I discussed in earlier chapters, I thank the good Lord that some great mentors taught me how to slow down and express myself. Now, I can talk to a person, and they will feel what I am feeling.

If you can do this, the recipient of your words will completely understand the feeling of the message you are communicating to them.

When I started running heavy equipment, I got a real quick education on the importance of correct communication. When you are operating heavy equipment on a construction site, you cannot just pull over the massive pieces of machinery and ask the other operator a question. And you especially cannot do that now since most heavy equipment is designed with closed cabs. Verbal communication just doesn't happen—unless you have a God-given voice like mine, loud enough to pierce any glass window.

LIFESAVING NON-VERBAL COMMUNICATION

Over the years, in the heavy construction industry, a slew of hand gestures, hand signals, and hand communication have replaced verbal communication to remedy hearing loss. The uncanny part is that when done right and understood by all, it is very effective.

For example, when running earthmoving scrapers, the grade setter, dump man, and even the foreman will flip their wrist and hand upward quickly, which means to the scraper operator, "Dump your load." Tapping the top of your hardhat means "Dump on top of the last pile or load." When a scraper operator opens both hands and brings them together in a big circle, it means, "I have a big rock in my load." Bringing your hand from your nose and dragging it down the center of your body means "Dump in the center."

Even telling time is a hand-gesture art. If you are trying to tell your crew that the shift will end at 5:30 p.m., simply hold up five fingers with your hand wide open, then pull your hand across your waist. That signifies a half amount. Presto! The whole crew knows you're quitting at 5:30 p.m.

Dozer operators running a cut will tap one of their shoulders to designate whether they want a scraper operator to set up on the left or right side and that they should start the loading process. A grade setter tapping his foot and holding up one, two, or three fingers signifies the depth of cut per foot. For instance, tapping your foot and holding up one finger means "There is one foot of material left to cut out."

When directing a loader operator on a wet utility crew, hitting your hardhat with your knuckles represents "Rock" or "I need you to bring me drain rock."

Crane operators and signalmen have an entire gambit of hand signals to follow when lifting or placing loads. Their position requires them to be exact, leaving no room for miscommunication or error. They must be right all the time, every time.

Knowing and understanding the hand signals mentioned above and paying attention to them can mean the difference between an operation's success and failure and its smooth flow. Smooth flow is the "Difference-Maker" in the construction world!

During my early education on the job site, I had no idea what all these hand signals meant. But I learned quickly that when they are not followed, it screws up the seamless flow of the entire operation. At lunch, I would get chewed out relentlessly because I was not following the proper hand signals. Basic comments were, "Morelock, you're dumber than dirt! Pay attention to the hand signals!" I so loved those comments! NOT!

The first signal I learned concerned an operator or foreman pointing their two fingers at their eyes, then pointing at me. That meant, "LOOK AT ME." I snapped to immediate attention when I saw that. They would then tell me what they wanted through a series of unknown gestures.

And, of course, I did know what the middle finger meant. I got that a lot in my early training.

Thumbs up meant "Good job;" thumbs down meant "You screwed up." I also got a lot of thumbs down.

However, once I started to master the knowledge and the importance of hand signals, my eyes were opened to the choreography and precise manipulation of a given operation. I understood all that could be achieved by a group of operators and laborers, working all day with hand signals and gestures while never verbally communicating during the dance. It was a marvelous thing to behold.

CHAPTER 7

TAKING EFFECTIVE COMMUNICATION TO THE NEXT LEVEL

"Of all the life skills available to us, communication is perhaps the most empowering."
—Bret Morrison

As I continued on in my career, it became more and more evident how vitally important good verbal communication is. It is one of the main components of success in this and any business. It is the Difference-Maker. It is the Game-Changer.

The better the communication, the better the performance, and the better the overall outcome of an operation or an entire project. I learned this lesson repeatedly. But I was determined to become a great communicator, and I was blessed to work with some damn good ones who have influenced how I address people today.

GIVING DETAILED DIRECTION—ALL THE TIME, EVERY TIME

One of my first major lessons in communicating and giving detailed directions all the time, every time, was when I was running a 637 Multi-Engine Scraper in a sand mine excavation. A team of 10 637 scrapers were working together as 5 2-man teams. The grading foreman was a master dirt mover. He knew his stuff. Let's call him Al. Unfortunately, as I was to soon learn, Al was a terrible communicator. He gave little or no direction in the morning meetings.

Al was very flat and bland in his delivery: "Just go here." "Dump there." "Get your asses moving." Al had a habit of stopping a team of scrapers and talking to the front or lead scraper operator for a minute, then jumping in his Jeep and driving away. The team he had talked to would immediately change up the entire operation. They might move to a different haul road, leading to a different cut and fill. Or they would reverse the haul pattern direction sometimes, which led to a few dangerous situations.

Meanwhile, the rest of the teams would continue with the initial operation they were involved with, oblivious to the changes the first team was implementing. This always led to complete chaos for about 10 minutes until everyone figured out that we were supposed to be doing something different.

Then Al would show up, yelling and screaming, throwing his arms around. During one of these tirades, when I was the lead scraper, he stopped me and started yelling about, "Why was I so stupid?" and "Can't you figure anything out, Morelock? What the hell is wrong with you?"

I was such a newbie that I just shut my mouth and took the verbal beating.

As Al drove off, I would shout to myself, *I can't read your mind, Al! Why don't ya just tell me what the hell you want in the first place!?*

It was evident that the rest of the scraper teams felt the same way. I always wondered why Al didn't just stop each team and let them know what was changing. Well, I got to learn the significance of this later in the work season when Al took some time off to go deer hunting.

A new excavation foreman was coming to the job site and taking over for the week while Al was gone. I couldn't wait to see how this new foreman would communicate with the crew.

The very first day with the new foreman was a meaningful learning experience. On that day, the foreman, who I'll call Steve, gathered all the operators around and went over the entire operations for the day. He explained everything he wanted the shift to accomplish in detail. It was incredible. The whole time, I stood there listening and thinking, *damn, this foreman is awesome. He really communicates and makes our jobs and mission for the day crystal clear.*

The meeting was dismissed, and off we went. To my continued amazement, during the shift, if Steve wanted to make a change, he stopped every team, one right after the other, and spoke to them for less than 30 seconds, explaining the change and what he wanted us to do.

As you can probably guess, the entire operation ran like, yes, the preferable Rolex watch. It was perfectly coordinated and organized. At the end of the shift, Steve would give everyone a high-5 and recognize the team's outstanding performance.

The funny thing was that he was the one orchestrating that outstanding performance. What a week it was! Morale went up; the tempo of the job increased, and we were moving dirt like a well-oiled machine.

The next Monday, Al showed up, bragging about his deer hunting trip, and everything returned to chaos. I saw the negativity in what he was doing. But I refused to engage. Instead, I looked at the positive side of what I had learned from Steve, and I carried that one-week education on the "Results of Effective Communication" with me right into the start of my own leadership career. What an eye-opener!! What a Game-Changer this was for me!

> *I went on to realize the utmost importance of giving detailed directions all the time, every time. Whether talking to a group or an individual, giving detailed directions is the only way to go.*

Make sure that what you are explaining or directing is precisely understood. Then, follow up consistently, so you are fully understood.

IT STARTED WITH DAD—"MAKE IT VISUAL"

The beauty of detailed direction is that it can come in both verbal and written form.

I grew up in the construction industry with my dad, who would always preach to me, "Son, a picture is worth a thousand words. Draw them a picture when you're trying to explain something. Let them see it, and let them feel it, and they will better understand it."

Of course, at 15 years old, working during the summer with my dad on an airport runway project in Prudhoe Bay, Alaska, I didn't really understand what he meant.

But, oh boy, when I became a foreman and then superintendent, my education on what Dad meant by "Draw them a picture" became dramatically clear.

In my heavy civil grading days, as a superintendent running a mass grading project, with the help of my key project foremen, I would bring out a blown-up poster of the project grading plan and lay it out wherever there was space—most often, my truck bed.

Giving the entire team the ability to "see the picture" opened their eyes and helped them visually understand what we were planning and explaining. The interaction was incredible. It underscored the significance of giving such detailed direction. From that day forward, I always ran my teams that way.

Later in my career, as a senior project manager, I continued to make damn sure that all the supervisors working with me took this thought process and ran with it. Our battle cry was, "Give Detailed Direction!" In other words, make sure what you are explaining is CRYSTAL CLEAR. Involve the team. Draw them a picture. Give them a step-by-step schematic. Make every effort to leave no stone unturned when giving directions. The buy-in and results are remarkable when you do this.

As a leader, always take the time to Give Detailed Direction. Anything less is unacceptable!

CHAPTER 8

MAKING THE TIME FOR "ONE-ON-ONE COMMUNICATION"

"The single biggest problem with communication is the illusion that it has taken place."
—George Bernard Shaw

One on One. Sounds like a good ol' pick-up game of basketball. You are close together with your opponent, trying to read their every step. You're watching their eyes and body movements to get the edge on them.

Confession: I was never really good at one-on-one matchups. My glasses always seemed to get in the way. Maybe I was trying to get too close. Regardless, they would get knocked off my face, and I'd get pissed off and have to start all over. That led to the brilliant idea of just taking off my glasses.

With my bare face, I would look my blurry opponent in the eye as best I could and think, *now, let's see what you got.* As you can imagine, that didn't go too far because I couldn't see anything. I was definitely no competition with glasses off. Even thinking about that memory makes me laugh.

Playing wide receiver on my high school football team and going up against the defensive ends went a little better. Now, my glasses were under my helmet, albeit constantly digging into my face and smashing up against my helmet, making it even harder to see. Thankfully, I did have a few pretty good moves, and I learned my own "one-on-one" ways to fake out the defender trying to keep me from catching the passes. Still, I was mostly miserable with my glasses under my helmet and never quite achieved the outcome I was working for.

Don't get me wrong. I didn't get the nickname "Freddie B." for nothing. As I stated in an earlier chapter, having my teammates refer to me as Fred Biletnikoff, the great wide receiver for the Oakland Raiders at that time, was a huge confidence builder for me! I even covered myself with "stick-um" to be just like him! I often wondered if contact lenses had been invented back then, what would my life have been like? Could I have made it to the NFL? Whatever the case, it just wasn't meant to be.

> *I was destined to learn that "one-on-one" had a whole different meaning than staring down an opponent with the eye of the tiger!*

ONE-ON-ONE COMMUNICATION—THE USEFULNESS OF GETTING PERSONAL

In the heavy construction trade, I quickly realized the absolute power and effectiveness of "one-on-one" communication.

As discussed earlier, my mentor, Herman Hall, was the master grade setter I was blessed to have the opportunity to work with early in my career. I spent hours each day with him, just the two of us, as I practiced reading plans and the art of grade layout. He was such a great teacher with unlimited patience.

I always went full bore and strove to go Mach 10 in everything. Herman taught me to slow down, be meticulous, and focus on the accuracy of my work versus the quantity of it. When it comes to grade layout in the civil grading world, accuracy is a must. Everything and everyone on the project are following the grade layout. If the stakes are wrong, elevations are wrong, cut and fill information is wrong, grade flagging is wrong, all the work completed is wrong.

This time I spent with Herman was priceless and marked a turning point in my career. The knowledge and communication he shared with me were instrumental in my future success.

Someday, when I get to Heaven, I can't wait to meet up with Herman and thank him for all his individual training and communication. It truly was priceless.

Next came additional one-on-one communication and training. My first salaried management job as a field superintendent and the one-on-one time I got with the project engineer was a career accelerator for me. The quality time he spent teaching me the project engineering side of the business helped accelerate my growth as a salaried manager. Of course, he had his hands full as I knew nothing about computers and takeoffs and didn't clearly understand specifications, tracking quantities, cost, etc. Without this engineer's help and personal approach, I may have never made it.

The list of people who have personally trained me is truly never-ending. All the in-depth, personal attention I received from my many mentors was incredible. It was as if I had my own panel of construction professors taking the time to teach me all they knew. This was the best of the best—effective, detailed, focused, almost intimate communication. Powerful.

As I moved forward in my career, I continued to personally learn, 100 times over, the power of one-on-one communication. Like my predecessors, I would spend countless quality hours working with a new supervisor to learn The Art of Being a Leader.

PAYING IT FORWARD

Now, I build quality relationships with my teams on the job in real time. I work to train them in how to communicate. In how to be patient with their team members. In how to talk to people on a personal level.

I teach them how to properly stop an equipment operator who is not doing what they want and understand why and how taking a few precious minutes to explain in detail what is going wrong and how to correct it is imperative.

After I give this instruction, I follow up with them, again, one-on-one to ensure they have fully understood and are learning and improving.

While doing this, I also have to train the new supervisor on the absolute importance of completely understanding the overall art of effective communication and how this must go hand-in-hand with "one-on-one" communication. You can't do one without the other if you want the Rolex watch to tick!

When I was a grading foreman, I stopped a fairly green scraper operator, pulled him off the rig, and explained his missteps and how to correct them. No matter who I was working with, I could always see the nervous look in their eyes. I knew they were worried we were wasting time. Earthmoving is a high-production game. Seconds and minutes are very costly. As the old adage goes, "Time is money." This is especially true on a mass grading scraper spread. Everything is measured in seconds. Seconds are precious.

I can recall many times when operators struggling with their technique would say, "Lonnie, just tell me what you want so I can get going." Bill was one of them.

We were excavating the Mehrten lava cap cut—very hard, rocky material. The work was difficult, and due to the extremely rocky terrain, certain methods had to be followed to be successful.

A new scraper tire back then was $7,000. To alleviate that maintenance cost and save tire wear, the team developed precise methods for dumping the loads.

They would come into the fill, shift their scraper into first gear as it sat just a little above the finished fill, and then, using the correct levers, crowd their load out as quickly as possible while driving off the edge of the fill. Then, they would shift their scraper back into automatic and drive off. This kept the rocky lava cap material in one spot for the dozers and compactors to work. No rocks were dribbled out across the fill area for the other scrapers to run over and cut and damage tires, either. As stated previously, scraper tires are VERY expensive!

In one instance, I pulled Bill aside, had him park his 651 Scraper, and asked him to stand and watch with me as the "seasoned" scraper hands entered the fill and dumped their load. I went through every detail of the dump step by step, asking him, "Bill, do you see how they are doing it? See how they downshift and quickly dump the load? It's smooth and even. See how they don't spill material all over the open ground in front of them?" Bill looked at me and said, "Wow, it looks so different from here on the ground. I can really see the technique." "Exactly," I replied. "We are communicating with our eyes."

I then had Bill get back up into the seat, and I climbed up and bent over on the cab floor. We went over how to manipulate the controls using a trick method to help crowd the material out of the can faster and smoother.

Bill hollered over the engine noise, "Damn, I never realized this was so easy!" I looked at him, smiled, and yelled back, "How could you know if no one ever took the time to show you?" He bellowed back, "No one ever has until now. I really want to thank you for taking the time now to show me. What a difference having someone personally show me the ropes. I really appreciate it, Lonnie!"

"Hey, no problem, Bill!" I clapped him on the shoulder and exclaimed, "Remember what you just learned here, and go and practice these techniques. You will catch on in no time! Time and money well spent, my man . . . . Time and money well spent."

And it definitely was.

That personalized time with Bill gave him one hell of a confidence booster. By the end of the shift, he was dumping like a pro. Bill went on to become one of our best scraper operators, working for us on many more projects.

Later that day, one of the other operators asked me, "Why did you take so much time with Bill? That was some expensive training. A lot of loads missed there! Hell, I would have just got his checks." Meaning that he would have fired him.

My answer was simple and to the point. "Who taught you? What is more effective? Taking a little one-on-one time to help the guy out and improve his skills and abilities and communicating and explaining things to him on a personal level that will also pay off down the road by having a dependable, seasoned operator on our team or just getting rid of him and hoping the next scraper hand we get out of the Union Hall will be better? I, for one, believe that the up-close-and-personal approach is way more beneficial!"

No matter who challenged me on the time I spent with the crew, when I explained my logic, the answer I got back was pretty much always the same. "Lonnie, I can't argue with that."

CHAPTER 9

PERSONAL TRAINING AT THE NEXT LEVEL

"If you are not willing to learn, no one can help you. If you are determined to learn, no one can stop you."
—Zig Ziglar

Last year, I was on a client's project, working with a new, young field supervisor. I had actually trained this same individual a few years ago as a key foreman. To my satisfaction, I learned that he had since been promoted and was learning the next level of field supervision as a project superintendent, advancing in his career as well deserved. He is super talented and has lots of ambition and the drive and passion to go with it. It all adds up to what I like to call "a win-win scenario"!

One day, mid-afternoon, I showed up on his job and found him stomping around like a wet hen. I could see immediately that he was agitated.

I calmly walked up and asked, "Hey, Dennis, what gives? Why the attitude this beautiful, productive day."

Oh boy, that set him off like a bottle rocket on the Fourth of July. It was as if he were just waiting for someone to come along and give him time to vent! He proceeded vehemently. "Art just isn't getting it. I mean, shit, he has been running that friggin' loader for almost two years now, and he just isn't getting any better. Look at this place. Looks like a bomb went off. Sanding the trench behind the lay crew is basic shit. Knocking down excavation spoils—basic shit. Creating access—basic shit! I would think by now he would have a handle on all of this!" Numerous vulgar expletives followed!! Fond memories of the "old Lonnie" quickly flashed through my mind. Go figure!

> *I calmly looked at him and replied in my best Dr. Phil voice, "Well, Dennis, have you ever spent any quality one-on-one time with him?"*

He turned to me, perplexed. "What the hell is one-on-one time? If you haven't noticed, I am trying to run a major underground project here, and I don't have time for holding hands and one-on-one togetherness."

I couldn't help but start laughing. Of course, that did not help with his moodiness.

Then, I looked him directly in the eye and stated, "Look, Dennis, part of your new role as a project superintendent is training your team. Now, we haven't gotten to that phase of your education just yet. That is coming. But until then, let me ask you this question: Why haven't you taken the small amount of time over the past two years to work with him personally? What do you think the advantage of that would be? You were and still are a top-notch production loader operator. That skill and talent, along with the many others you have, is what got you promoted to foreman in the first place. Have you ever shared your knowledge, talents, and abilities at running a loader with Art?"

88

Dennis scowled at me and said, "And please tell me, when do I have the time for that? Look around. You know, if anybody knows, I have a lot going on out here. Where do I find the time for that, oh, great trainer dude!?"

When I finished cracking up once more, I could sense that the air of arrogance and frustration in my pupil was passing. I calmly replied, "Dennis, I know, as you well know, the daily difficulty faced by a field supervisor running a project. But if you never take the time to train your team members, to help them improve their distinct skills and abilities for the job they are performing as part of your team, how will they get better, and subsequently, how will your overall team get better? Remember, my young Jedi, the whole aspect of Continuous Improvement does not just apply to you developing your field leadership skills. An integral part is developing your entire team. You have to share your knowledge and abilities with them so they can learn and improve right along with you. Like I have told you many times, 'A rising tide floats all boats.' The never-ending goal is to continuously improve. And that applies to both you and your team. As you work to improve them, they will improve at the same time! It's a beautiful concept."

Dennis shrugged and replied, "I'm picking up what you're throwing down. I just struggle with finding the time."

"You have to find the time."

Then, I grinned and let him in on my plan. "I'll tell you what I am going to do. I will be here at startup time tomorrow. I will spend all day with Art one-on-one. I will work with him all day long, all over the job site, as he performs his role as a production loader operator. I will follow him like a little lost puppy. By the end of the day, let's see what happens. You good with that?"

Dennis turned and said, "I guess I will have to be. You're the trainer. I can't wait to see how this is done." I didn't miss the sarcastic tone in his voice, but I ignored it. "Cool," I replied. "Then it's a date with Art."

I was so excited! Oh, how I was looking forward to helping Dennis expand his mind. Tomorrow couldn't come soon enough.

ONE-ON-ONE AND THEN SOME

The next day came, and as usual, I was on the job bright and early, ready to bring my A-game in working with Art. I met up with Dennis, who proceeded to explain everything Art was responsible for in a day. In all honesty, when this first went down, Art was not too pleased with what was transpiring.

I took Art off to the side and gave him the lowdown. "Look, Art," I started calmly and directly, "you are a good loader hand. But there are a lot of different skills you have yet to learn. Just give me your full, undivided attention today. Work with me all day long in all that I will 'show and tell' you on improving your overall loader operating skills. Then, let's see how you feel by the end of the day. Do we have a deal?"

Art dropped his head and grudgingly agreed. He walked off to his loader, and I followed.

I could tell that Art felt like he was getting this extra attention because he wasn't good enough and was doing a bad job. He would soon learn how far from the truth his current thought process concerning his ability was. He was a good loader operator. He just needed a little TLC to improve his skills and talent!

I spent the entire shift following Art all through the project. I schooled him on everything I had learned as a production loader operator back in my equipment operating days. He got instruction on how to work the bucket like an extension of his very own hand, how to knock down trench spoils properly and build access for the pipe crews without getting material in the excavated trenches. He learned the right way to dump sand and rock into the trench, working without a spotter and using his wheel tracks to keep him centered and in the correct position for backfilling the open trenches, clean and evenly. I would stop him frequently, take him off the loader, and spend a few minutes detailing different techniques and approaches.

After lunch, I took Art into my truck, and we traveled throughout the project site. I taught him how to manage his time in different locations and stay on top of where the different crews needed him at different times.

Art learned the art of managing the aggregate trucks hauling materials to the project and showed them where to dump piles at specific locations for ease of access to the work areas and optimum productivity. I gave him all I had for a full eight hours. The entire time, I could see Dennis watching me. That was a good thing.

At the end of the shift, Art parked his loader, dismounted the machine, and walked up to me very humbly. He took my hand and started shaking it. Tears welled up in his eyes. He tried to talk, but he couldn't form the words yet. I patted him on the shoulder and said, "Hey, Art, it's all good."

He stared at me almost in disbelief and murmured, "No, Lonnie, it's not all good. I know my attitude really sucked this morning. I was a little pissed off and a little too full of myself. I was like, *what is this guy going to teach me*? I can't believe all that I have learned today. Absolutely incredible. What a day! Man, what a day!"

I gave him a big ol' bear hug and said, "Art, I got to be where I am today because my mentors took the time early in my career to work one-on-one with me to teach and train me. That is all I have done with you. I am just passing on the knowledge."

Art said a little too loudly, "Why hasn't anyone here on the job ever given me this time? I know Dennis was a badass loader hand back in the day, but he's never taught me anything. I've just had to learn on my own so far."

I smiled warmly and said, "Art, we all have different things we need to work on. Dennis is working on improving his team training skills. I think, no, I know that today will be a real eye-opener for him. We all strive to continuously improve every minute, of every hour, of every day. As your skills improve, as your abilities continue to grow, you will someday share all your knowledge with a new, young, inexperienced loader hand."

Art was smiling now.

I went on, "It is a revolving door that never closes, and it should never close."

Art replied with another smile, "Right on, Lonnie. Thank you so much. I am going to work my ass off tomorrow, implementing all the new shit you taught me today. I am going to be the best damn loader hand this company has ever seen! Thank you. Thank you so much. You're the man!"

I gave Art one last big hug, and he turned to walk back to his crew just finishing up for the day.

As I headed back to my truck, Dennis wasted no time getting to me. He walked up, hanging his head like a whipped puppy. Then, looking up at me, he said, "Wow, just f_____g wow! What a difference. Where has my head been?"

I looked at him and firmly said, "Dennis, your head has been involved in learning how to be a project superintendent. You have come a long way, but you have a long way to go. I just spent eight hours with Art. Now, ask yourself honestly, how much time over just this past work season could you have spent one-on-one with Art? Possibly just one hour a day?"

Dennis glanced at me, then stared off in the distance. "Well, after seeing you in action today, I could have worked with him plenty of times. I guess I didn't have my priorities right."

I responded, "It's not all about priorities, Dennis. It's about helping your people, under your supervision, to become the absolute best they can be. Which then, in turn, helps *you* become the best that you can be. That is the recipe for Performance Above & Beyond. That is the recipe for achieving Absolute Teamwork. Now, moving forward, continue to expand on all I have taught Art today. You have spent way more time on a production loader than I ever did. You are super knowledgeable on the techniques of running a production loader on a wet utilities pipe crew. I would venture to guess that you have a lot more to show and teach him than I can. Keep your focus on continuing to help him. Spend quality time with him when he needs further instruction. Do this, and six months from now, he will blow your mind!"

"Right on, Lonnie," he exclaimed. "I got it. See you next week!"

Six months later, I was on another huge underground project that Dennis was supervising. It would be one of his most successful projects of the year. He and his team were making shit happen and working together like the Rolex watch I always talk about.

The project owner's rep was absolutely thrilled. I sat in my truck for a bit and watched Art in action. In pure construction lingo, "He was making that loader sing." The entire team was dancing. The production levels were off the charts.

Dennis drove up to my truck with a big, broad smile. "You likin' what you're seeing, Obi-Wan? Are we kicking ass, or what? This is sooooo sweet! I really love how this feels!"

Now, it was my turn for the words to escape me. I quickly turned my head so he could not see my eyes watering. I was so damn proud of him.

I stared off for a minute, taking it all in before turning back to him. "Dennis, this is exactly where I knew you would get to. You should be very proud of your performance and your team. You are really making it happen! Just friggin' awesome!" Dennis got out of his truck, walked over to my rolled-down window, and put his hand on my arm. "No, Lonnie," he replied, "You made it happen. You opened my eyes. There was so much I wasn't seeing. But I sure as hell am starting to see it now."

I shot him one last smile, put my truck in gear, and said, "Dennis, I just showed you the way. You took it and ran with it. This is all you, my brother. Every single bit of this is all you! Now, what is the next step?"

Dennis replied without missing a beat, "Keep on communicating and improving!"

I gave him a big wink, a nod of my head, and drove away! When I checked my rearview mirror, Dennis was blowing me kisses. I thought to myself, *okay, now, let's not get carried away . . .* as tears of pride and satisfaction streamed down my cheeks.

Throughout my career as a project supervisor, no matter my level, I continued to hone my craft of one-on-one communication. Whether in the office or the field, taking the time to really connect, train, and teach was a Game-Changer, a Difference-Maker, and, yes, a money-maker.

Most importantly, it's exhilarating watching individuals grow in their respective careers and help them be all they can be with a personal approach.

I came to realize that although being a builder was awesome, fun, exciting, and rewarding, there was more. Nothing compares to building and developing people. That is the icing on the cake with the cherry on top.

It is priceless.

No matter who you are working with on your team, whether a new supervisor, a member of your office staff, a craft employee, or even a brand-new hire, always find and take the time for one-on-one mentoring, coaching, training, and teaching.

THE DIVIDENDS ARE ENDLESS AND WILL CONTINUE TO PAY OFF FOR YEARS TO COME!

CHAPTER 10

TEAM COMMUNICATION: BEING "IN THE KNOW"

"Good communication is the bridge between confusion and clarity."
—Nat Turner

Is everyone on your team "In the Know?" Yes, I have constantly asked my team, "Hey, am I keeping you 'In the Know?'"

Damn, what does that Lonnieism even mean? Well, in the never-ending vernacular of Lonnieisms, it means that every single member of the team knows exactly what is going on all the time. Each and every member of the team thoroughly understands the plan, where we are going, and what it is going to take to get there. No question. There is no wondering about what is going on or what is going to happen. There is only 100% understanding and comprehension of the day's and/or week's activities. Being "In the Know" also includes goals, scheduled milestones, productivity goals, operational goals, and overall achievement goals.

When I first started running work, I had no clue what keeping my crew "In the Know" really meant. I had not coined the phrase yet because, as discussed in earlier chapters, I was just learning the art of communication and how to be a good leader. I had a hard enough time just keeping myself "In the Know." There was so much information to comprehend and so much information to share!

How was I to communicate this plethora of never-ending information?

What was the most pertinent information for my team to know at any given time?

What was the most important information for the shift or the week?

It didn't seem like planning for a month out was reasonable. It was an eternity, as I thought about it. I wondered *how do I communicate a month out?! It seems utterly impossible*!

As I progressed in my career as a field leader, I began to understand what being "In the Know" meant. It could encompass a one-day activity that needed to be thoroughly communicated to everyone involved in that specific activity. It could encompass communication with multiple crews—all involved in completing the same operation. It could encompass a plan for the entire week. There were many things it could mean.

It depended on the given time of the project, who was or would be involved, and the required level of overall communication.

Trying to figure out how to relay all this information to the entire team was a real challenge for me.

My dilemma with sharing a plethora of information made a complete turnaround for the better at one early morning start-up meeting on one of my first really huge mass-grading projects.

It went down like this.

I was attempting to review the day's plan with the crew. It was not going well. In fact, it was going horribly! I could tell the crew members were frustrated.

I called out one of my key foremen and said, "Hey Ron, how 'bout 'splaining' to these gents what is on our minds?" He looked at me like he had seen a ghost. *Uh-oh, bad idea.* Finally, one of the key dozer operators, Jason, exclaimed, "How 'bout just draw us a freaking picture. A diagram. Anything that we can look at instead of waving arms and pointing fingers."

> *The lightbulb immediately went off in my very annoyed head. A drawing, a schematic, full-scale, large-sized. BIG! BOLD!*

As a first quick remedy, I pulled out the overall grading plan sheet, threw it on the bed of my company truck, and gathered everyone around. It wasn't perfect, but it was a start.

I drew a big "X" like the ones on a shopping mall map with all the different store locations that tell you, "YOU ARE HERE." I then went on to draw the cut and fill areas for the shift, explaining where we would start and end the day.

WOW! What a mind-blower.

The crew loved it.

Now, that may seem like a very simple example of getting your team "In the Know" of what is going on, but it was a start.

With the help of several of my key foremen, I went on to develop full-sized colored schematics of the project to share the game plan for the day. It was a huge success!

The turnaround in sharing large amounts of information with the crew continued to evolve!

We might start with 20-30 operators all standing around at the beginning of the shift; then, by using a 4-ft. by 8-ft. picture diagram, they could all see and completely understand what was being reviewed. Every single crewmember walked away from that meeting thoroughly "In the Know" of what was going on.

If the plan from the morning shift changed after the lunch break, we utilized the same approach.

Everyone's goal was to understand their role on the team, where they belonged, and what they were supposed to do.

The phrase "In the Know" became our motto, leading us to the coveted "promised land" of Performance Above & Beyond and Absolute Teamwork!

CHAPTER 11

A THEATRICAL APPROACH TO COMMUNICATION EDUCATION

"The more we learn about effective communication, the better we will be at leading, as our directives will be better understood."
—Paul Jarvis

One of the best ways to get across the importance of communication is through storytelling and sharing common experiences we can all relate to.

I like movies. Movies can be great leadership teachers when you allow the content to take you down that path.

You know by now that I am a "guy-flick" movie buff. There's nothing like a great movie, especially one that reflects leadership and includes leadership training scenarios that come alive.

In this next section, I am sharing some communication learning opportunities I picked up while watching a few of my favorite all-time movies.

Yes, there is a long list of my favorite movies, starting with John Wayne, Clint Eastwood, old Western movies, and war and adventure movies. There are also a few really good love stories, aka "tear jerkers."

The first one that comes to mind in that category is *Where the Red Fern Grows,* detailing the love of a boy and his two hunting dogs. That one is a gut-wrencher. My wife would have a different opinion on what constitutes a love story and would argue the likes of *The Notebook,* among others. That movie is the standing love story reference in our home!

We can't forget the more modern-day theatrical blockbusters like *Top Gun, Mission Impossible, Raiders of the Lost Ark*, and on and on.

Those are notable, sure, but a distinct few have some great teachable leadership moments that cause me to reflect on what I've learned long after the movie is over.

I will focus on these few examples in the following pages. If you have seen the movies and scenes I am relating, you will know exactly where I am coming from.

If you haven't seen these movies, don't worry. You can still follow along. I will highlight what you need to know. But first, before we get started, I have to say that my heart goes out to you as you have really been missing out. Now . . . go watch the friggin' movies!

Regardless of what camp you fall into, my hope is that you get a new sense and understanding of these teachable leadership moments and utilize them to continue to help you in your quest to know and understand "What Makes Your Team Tick?"

It's curtain time!

HOW TO BRING YOUR FEELINGS TO YOUR COMMUNICATION— MOVIE STYLE!

When it comes to sharing feelings through communication, the best movie analogy I can give you is the movie *Braveheart* with Mel Gibson, starring as William Wallace. When he talked to his clansmen about Scotland's freedom from the oppression of England, everyone felt a stirring in their souls. The men and women standing before him grew to share his conviction and desire to be free. He was brave and courageous and lived with the burning anger inside to avenge the killing of the love of his life by the evil noblemen who served the King of England.

But his belief in obtaining freedom from England was his true driver.

If you have seen the movie, you know the outcome. After many battles fought and dealing with tyranny and traitors within his own people, he was captured and ordered to be put to death by the King of England, who was a very unpleasant individual!

This king needed a lot of leadership training. The Scottish freedom fighters were downcast over William Wallace's capture. The clans splintered, and many felt beaten. Yet, as Mel Gibson, "Braveheart," lay on a table getting gruesomely tortured to death, he never pleaded for mercy. He said NOTHING!

Then, just as he was about to be put to death, having endured the savage pain of his torture, he screamed the famous word, "FREEDOM," at the top of his lungs.

The tale of his bravery and conviction spread like wildfire among the Scottish clansmen aligned with him and even touched the cowards who had betrayed him. Every living soul who heard his scream of freedom was moved by his greatness and undeniable, intense emotions. He filled the hearts of the Scottish people. So much so that they rallied together and won their freedom from England by defeating their army in a major battle. Scotland became a sovereign nation. I can't answer if that was truly and historically accurate, but for our purposes, it doesn't matter.

> *The level of "feeling" in the communication of freedom from the heart and soul of William Wallace was powerful, and it changed the course of history.*

When you are trying to rally your team to achieve the unachievable or helping a direct report clearly understand what you want to teach them, letting them FEEL what you are communicating can make the difference in their success.

> *Let your guard down a little bit. Give it a try. Let them feel you. You will love the results.*

COMMUNICATING & TRAINING THROUGH ALLOWED FAILURE

The question you are asking yourself, that I am feeling right about now, is, "Lonnie, what the hell do you mean by communicating training through allowed failure?" In my perfectly blunt way, I mean exactly what the statement suggests. As a leader, there are times when you must permit a team member or direct report the opportunity to fail completely at a task.

You will know well in advance that they are going to fail, but still, you let them fail because it will teach them a great lesson.

This can be difficult, and it takes incredible patience. But in certain times and places, it is so effective. When someone learns through failure, the lesson learned stays with them for the rest of their career and/or the rest of their life. I have learned many great lessons this exact way, dating all the way back to my early days as a heavy equipment operator and all the way up to my days as a senior manager.

> *Great mentors allow us to learn through the communication of failure.*

Another one of my all-time favorite movies, *Jeremiah Johnson*, is a perfect example of this concept.

Not only does this movie tell a great story of survival, willpower, loyalty, love, revenge, and redemption, but it also contains some outstanding leadership-teaching moments. I get chills just thinking about it. Keep reading, and you will see exactly where I am going.

Early in the movie, Robert Redford, aka Jeremiah Johnson, leaves the Civil War. All the death and destruction he had witnessed filled him with the desire to escape civilization and the hatred of man, so he set out to disappear into the rugged, lonely wilderness of the Rocky Mountains and become a mountain man.

His first experiences end in disaster, with him nearly starving and freezing to death. He realizes that he definitely needs to learn how to fish!

When he is almost at the end of his rope, he stumbles across Will Geer, aka Bear Claw Chris Lapp, a rugged, well-seasoned expert at living off the land and hunting Grizzly Bears. Bear Claw befriends Jeremiah and takes him under his wing to teach him how to be a mountain man and all he knows about survival in the Rockies.

> *At one point in Jeremiah's training, he and Bear Claw are in a remote area getting ready to bed down for the night. All the snow on the ground makes it one cold son-of-a-bitch.*

Just the thought of lying down in the snow and sleeping in be-low-zero temperatures makes me realize that if I were in Jeremiah Johnson's shoes, I would need to take my camping skills to the next level. I think I will stick to a nice warm tent and a down sleeping bag!

As the movie continues, Bear Claw shows Jeremiah how to keep warm at night. He teaches him how to dig a pit in the ground big enough to lie down in. Then, he is to fill the pit with large rocks from around the campfire that have been super-heated. He then demonstrates how to cover the rocks with a layer of dirt and pine tree branches to make a nice, warm, cushy bed. Sounds so comfort-able, doesn't it?

All is well, and they lay down to go to sleep.

Then everything goes rapidly downhill for Jeremiah. In the mid-dle of the night, he screams in terror and tries to leap out of his rock-warmed bed, his blankets and clothes smoking and on fire. He stumbles out of the makeshift bed, bellerin' at the top of his lungs, desperately trying to free himself from the smoking hot blankets and his steaming hot clothes. Ol' Bear Claw Chris Lapp calmly rolls over in his perfectly warm bed and softly says, "Ya, I saw it right off. You didn't put enough dirt down."

Jeremiah is pissed beyond belief. Bear Claw almost got him burned up in his sleep! The moral of this story and the training exer-cise embedded in this movie is that Bear Claw knew well in advance that Jeremiah *had not* watched him carefully as to how he was in-structing him in making a warm bed.

Jeremiah did not watch *just exactly* how much dirt Bear Claw placed over his hot rocks to protect him from their intense heat. He did not appreciate that he needed enough dirt covering to allow for the warmth from the super-heated rocks to keep him snuggly and warm all night and that that layer needed to be thick enough to protect him from cooking!

Bear Claw knew what was going to happen as he watched Jeremiah prepare his bed. He knew well in advance that Jeremiah was going to burn his ass off. Now, Bear Claw could have chewed out Jeremiah or laughed and told him how stupid he was. But he did not do that. He handled it perfectly.

He ALLOWED Jeremiah to learn from his mistake. He knew he needed to learn from his failure without reprimanding and ridiculing him. What a great leadership training lesson! What great communication in failure.

Although it may have been painful for Bear Claw to watch the lesson transpire, he knew that letting Jeremiah learn from his failure assured he would never make the same mistake again.

In the future, Jeremiah would always be able to protect himself from the elements. He would have a restful night's sleep in a nice warm bed because he knew better.

Jeremiah went on to gain great respect and admiration for Bear Claw Chris Lapp, and he always knew that Bear Claw had the best intentions in mind when training him on the skills and talents of being a successful mountain man. Later in the movie, Bear Claw and Jeremiah Johnson cross paths again, and when they do, Jeremiah is sitting in a warm bed by a fire, cooking rabbit.

Bear Claw sits down, and the first thing he says after all the years that have passed between them is, "You've come far, pilgrim." The gleam in his eyes and the smile on his face at the pride he feels for Jeremiah says it all.

In that moment, Bear Claw knows that Jeremiah has become a highly skilled and competent mountain man. He knows that allowing him to learn from failure has paid off.

Great lesson. Great movie.

Communication to Build Confidence— The Art of Empathy

In this example, let's take a look at the movie *The Abyss*. It's an awesome science fiction adventure movie that really stretches the mind and imagination. And even though it's a guy flick, there's a bit of a love story thrown into the mix.

In one particular scene in the movie, Ed Harris, aka Bud Brigman, one of the leaders in this saga, is about to descend into the unknown depths and darkness of the abyss to locate a nuclear weapon that has been lost due to the antics of a rouge Navy SEAL.

This nuclear weapon, if not deactivated, could destroy and/or wipe out a potential underwater alien civilization. If that happens, it will also kill all the current survivors on the crippled oil rig.

Captain Bud Brigman dons a state-of-the-art deep-water suit, allowing him to breathe liquid oxygen, similar to what we take in as babies in our mother's womb. This is highly classified military equipment, which hasn't really been tested, but he's going for it anyway. This suit also supposedly protects the human body against the intense pressures of the deepest depths of the ocean. Bud Brigman is all set to jump off a vertical underwater cliff and sink into the unknown depths of the sea, where no man has gone before. Pretty hairy! But Bud is a savage; he knows he has to get this done to save all members of these civilizations. He has no choice.

You need to know that throughout the show, Bud Brigman has run-ins with his technical engineer, who also happens to be his estranged wife, Lindsey, played by Mary Mastrantonio. She is a real firebrand. In other words, not a very nice person. Even saying that describes her gently. Honestly, she is a full-on witch 99% of the time, and everyone knows it.

However, at this point in the movie, she and Bud Brigman are rekindling their romance, especially since Bud has just saved her life after she nearly drowned. Also, Bud never stopped loving her. He's always loved her.

As the story unfolds, Bud has the deep-water suit on and is breathing liquid oxygen. (I would love to try that someday.) Bud walks out onto the ocean floor and into the icy waters of the deep. He stops at the edge of the abyss and peers down into the black, mysterious darkness before leaping off the ledge. As he falls into the black unknown, surrounded by nothing but darkness, he is so alone.

But he can't talk because he is breathing liquid oxygen, although the suit has an intercom for communication. He can hear the voices of his comrades in the control center of the crippled oil rig, so he knows he isn't truly alone.

Lisa, aka "One Night Stand," played by Kimberly Scott, instructs Lindsey to talk to Bud to keep him focused. Lindsey chats at Bud like one of the workers. She gives away absolutely no feeling but prattles on in a "get the job done" manner.

Lindsey's heart is breaking as Bud plummets into the unknown. Then he starts losing it as the pressure of the deep gets to him. He flails about with uncontrollable spasms. It looks like everything is "going to hell in a handbasket." In other words, the mission may be doomed.

Lisa then softly whispers to Lindsey, the witch from hell: "Lindsey, just talk to him. Lindsey, really talk to him." Lindsey gets the point immediately from the feeling of Lisa's communication. She changes her tone and talks to Bud with deep care and concern. She reassures him and gently says, "I love you, Bud," as she insists everything will be alright. In a heartfelt, loving, and caring way, she gets through to him! Bud responds accordingly. Through the feeling of her communication, he regains his confidence and composure. He realizes he *is* up to the task at hand, and nothing is going to stop him. Most importantly, he wants to get back to Lindsey!

Bolstered by hearing that he is cared for and that people have confidence in him, he lands right on top of the missing nuclear bomb, dismantles it perfectly, and saves the day.

I don't want to spoil the rest of the movie because it is pretty damn awesome and amazing. However, the training moment in this example is and should be completely understandable. Lindsey communicates her emotion that Bud should have self-confidence, and he feeds off her faith and belief in him. As he hears her heartfelt communication, his confidence level shoots through the roof.

Moral of this story: When one of your team members is struggling, when they do not believe in themselves or their abilities, you must, as the leader, communicate self-confidence to them. Communicate with feeling! Show them empathy. Show them that you really, truly care about them and their personal development. You must find the words of encouragement that will give them the kick in the butt they need to fulfill their duty. Communicating confidence is a Difference-Maker, especially when whoever you are infusing your belief into truly feels and acts upon it!

Be a confident communicator and watch your team shine like the morning sun!

Communication to Share Your Opinion

Next, I will use a definite love story adventure to make this point. In this great movie, *The Man from Snowy River*, Harrison, played by Kirk Douglas, is a wealthy cattle rancher who has built his empire with the hard work and sweat of his hands. You can probably quickly figure out that he is an accomplished, arrogant bastard who thinks his "you-know-what" doesn't stink. Clancy, played by Jack Thompson, is a professional cowboy of the time, a living legend, famous throughout all the land for his expertise with horses and cattle. Jim Craig, played by Tom Burlington, is the son of a poor, deceased farmer/rancher who lives in a small, ramshackly house high in the rugged outback mountains of Australia.

Yes, the movie is supposed to take place in Australia. Jim Craig's dream is to follow his father's dream and have a successful ranch someday high up in the mountains where he grew up.

Jim has taken a job on Harrison's cattle ranch and, along the way, has fallen in love with his gorgeous daughter. In the scene I am referring to, Harrison, Harrison's sister, Clancy, and Harrison's lawyer are all sitting around a table having dinner and talking about the future.

Harrison is boasting about how he wants to figure out a way to send beef to America, to enlarge his kingdom and profit margins. He gets into an argument with Clancy concerning growing the ranch and taking over more territory by "taming the mountains," i.e., "getting rid of all the farmers and small ranchers who live up there." About that time, Jim walks in with an armload of firewood to add to the fireplace in the dining room. Clancy asks Jim his opinion on all of this. Jim Craig doesn't miss a beat. He speaks with wisdom and authority, saying, "You might as well try to hold back the tides as try to tame the mountains."

Jim doesn't say another word. He just puts the wood down and walks out. Everyone at the table is silent. Dumbfounded. They sit there in awe at the prophetic words that the young Jim Craig has just spoken. In that small sentence, the power of Jim's words pierces all their hearts and minds. For an instant, you can almost see them trying to picture someone or something attempting to hold back the tides of the ocean. They realize that Jim is right. There is no "taming the mountains." That is never going to happen, and they all know it. Harrison knows it!

When communicating your opinion on a subject, you need to slow down, formulate your thoughts, and generate a response that the people or individuals you are talking to can "'feel'" and completely understand without any doubt—just like Jim Craig.

Communicating your opinion in a logical, authoritative manner can change minds and outcomes. When people clearly understand your opinion, they can formulate thoughts based on the education you gave them. Problems or issues that couldn't be solved or resolved before can be solved and resolved. Everyone gets on the same page. The opinion is crystal clear.

Most importantly, everyone understands exactly where you are coming from, so there is no deviation in anyone's mind or thought process. That's because you have given them no gray areas to argue.

Communicating this way means collaboration begins anew, and the team gets back on track. Communicate to share your opinion with deep feeling and clarity. People around you will respond accordingly, and most of the time, quite positively!

COMMUNICATING TO BOLDLY SHARE YOUR VISION AND MISSION

This final example is another one of my favorites. In my experience in the world of leadership, team building, training, overcoming adversity, problem-solving, and on and on and on, this movie may provide the best example of all.

It explains the difference between monumental success and dismal failure and how it is all wrapped around correctly communicating your vision and mission.

Companies have a vision statement, which turns into a mission statement. You should also have a vision for your team and a vision for your life. How you share these visions is always the Difference-Maker. You have to be able to communicate your vision and share it so strongly that the people you are involved with will want to follow you exactly where you want them to go. They will want to follow you on your mission!

The goal is to get them to follow you with unbridled commitment, loyalty, and enthusiasm. Your vision sets the course for the ship you are sailing. Your team will then take that vision and set the sails. Your vision puts the wind in the sails. It pushes you forward on the course you want to travel. It gets you to your final destination successfully! It fulfills your mission!

With that thought in mind, let's examine my all-time favorite movie based on a real-life story. It concerns a famous British explorer of the early 1900s, Ernest Shackleton. Ernest sets out on a voyage in 1914 with his ship and hand-picked crew to be the first humans on Earth to reach the South Pole of Antarctica.

If he makes it, it will be a monumental achievement, a victory for the British crown, and it will solidify Ernest's place in history as one of the greatest explorers of all time. The movie is titled *Shackleton* and stars Kenneth Branagh. It is spectacularly awesome and amazing all at once.

Unfortunately, partway through the movie, Ernest's ship encounters severe weather and locks up in an Antarctic ice floe. The Shackleton expedition to the South Pole ends abruptly. The mission is a failure. The ship is frozen in the ice and eventually crushed by the extreme force of the shifting ice. The entire crew has to abandon it. They are thousands of miles away from anywhere or anything.

In the freezing Antarctic cold, Shackleton has only one option: trek across miles of ice in unknown and unchartered territory and try to reach help at a whaling station on Elephant Island so his crew and he can be rescued. This movie and the book *Shackleton's Way* might be one of the greatest leadership stories of all time; it demonstrates how to communicate "vision" exceptionally well.

At one point in their trek to the station, one of the crew members commits borderline mutiny. He doesn't believe in Shackleton anymore, and he doesn't want to follow orders anymore, either. This is when Shackleton shares his unstoppable vision to get all of them to safety. He scolds the potential mutineer and tells him flat out, "If you do what I say, I will keep you alive!" This is a turning point in the movie.

Shackleton shares his vision emphatically with his crew. He lets them know that his vision is to get every single one of them home safely and that he will not allow any of them to die or not make it home. His vision is strong and all-consuming.

He relentlessly communicates what must be done. His men must understand him, and they do. Everyone realizes his vision. They sense and feel it. Then they band together, following his vision every day and night through unprecedented hardship. Ernest's vision gives them strength and endurance. It allows them to persevere in the face of relentless, horrendous conditions. His vision gives them hope.

And where there is hope, there is desire. And where there is desire, there is performance. And where there is performance, there is achievement.

It's all driven by vision. His vision. Ernest has constantly communicated and shared his vision in the face of never-ending adversity, and his ability to continuously communicate and share it leads to the rescue of the entire crew.

After 18 months of non-stop hell, his vision gets them home. Ernest Shackleton may not have gone down in history as a legendary explorer—but he was. He did go down in history as one of the greatest leaders of all time! As I watched this movie, I couldn't forget that his vision made the impossible happen. Watch the movie, read the book, and learn the power of communicating and sharing your vision.

As I look back on my life, the men and women I have worked with, and the challenging teams I have had the privilege to lead and be associated with, I always attribute every success I have achieved to correctly communicating and sharing my vision.

One of the greatest definitions of a leader comes from a quote by Dwight D. Eisenhower: "Leadership is getting people to follow you in the direction that you want them to go because they want to." This quote is the epitome of communicating and sharing your vision.

Try communicating and sharing your vision with your team. Let them feel it. Let them smell it. Let them taste it. Let them reach out and almost touch it. I assure you, then, and only then, will they follow you in the direction you want them to go.

Success will follow close behind!

The art of effective communication is a never-ending learning process.

As we grow in our lives and careers, we never quit learning how to communicate better. But as we improve our communication skills, our ability to correctly express ourselves improves as well. The better we get at getting across what we feel, the better the result of what we are trying to accomplish with ourselves and our teams.

Constantly practice and improve your communication skills to learn "What Makes Your Team Tick," and before you know it, you will have your answers.

NOW, GO GET 'EM!

CHAPTER 12

SHOW THEM YOU TRULY CARE

"Take care of your people, and they will take care of you."
—Lonnie S. Morelock, 2024

In my first few experiences as a project foreman and project superintendent, I learned some very valuable lessons from previous supervisors about showing people you truly care. Unfortunately, this was demonstrated to me in a very negative way!

But I learned from it, and that's what matters.

When I finally became a fairly competent grade setter, I was in charge of maintaining all the cut-and-fill slope staking on a large, new freeway project.

The job stretched out for approximately three miles up and over a set of foothills. I would start chasing the scrapers in the cuts at the beginning of the day, laying out the ongoing excavations, and then later on in the workday, I would move to the fill to keep up on all the staking and layout of the fill slopes. Due to the company safety policies at the time, my personal truck, which I used as my work truck, was not allowed on the job site. I always had to park in the designated crew parking locations.

In the early morning, I would put on my tool bags and gather all my gear, and then the project foreman would give me a ride to my starting location for the shift. By lunchtime, I was always, invariably, quite a fair distance from my truck, which, of course, had my lunch box containing gobs of good stuff.

I've always loved having a gourmet lunch. Ice cold water or Gatorade was my daily drink of choice, and I enjoyed a good supply of candy. For energy, of course! I wish I could still eat like that!

As the story goes, I would see the scraper operators, blade hands, etc., heading back to the crew parking lot, and I knew it was lunchtime. So, I would drop my bags and climb up or walk down to the haul roads, depending on where I was at that given moment.

Then the project foreman would speed my way, and whoosh, he would blow right past me. Hey, he was on an important mission, heading offsite to get his lunch! I would wave wildly at him, exclaiming to myself, *here I am. Stop. Give me a ride back to my truck. Hey! Hey! See me. Here I am . . . .* But this man wouldn't even give me the time of day! All that was on his mind was getting to the burger joint or wherever he went for lunch. I was so pissed, and now, I had to walk all the way back to my truck, which generally took about 10-15 minutes.

To add insult to injury, this was normally during the hottest summer months, meaning it was a balmy 95-plus degrees. With no other choices, I would trek back to my truck, grab my lunch, plop down on the ground, lean up against a tire, and wolf down my lunch. I only had precious minutes left of the 30-minute lunch period before I had to get back to work. This happened time and time again. I never said anything. I never complained.

But boy, oh boy, did I always lament under my breath, *what a complete asshole! He doesn't give two shits about* me. I told myself *when I become a foreman, I will never treat my guys this way, never!*

I've witnessed this kind of uncaring behavior often in my career as a craft employee, project foreman, and on through the ranks. All kinds of supervisors never really gave a damn about the people working for them. They didn't care about the people out there on the job site, giving their all for the overall success of the project. They never went the extra mile to help and support them. It was always all about them. In my mind, this was, and still is, totally unacceptable.

In my field leadership development training now, I get the opportunity to share these stories with my trainees. I implore that the better they treat their people, the harder they will work for them. Understand, being good to your team should never be the reason to get them to perform. It is just common courtesy. Treating them with dignity, honor, and respect should be the standard . . . all the time!

When your people know you truly, genuinely care about them, that you are always looking out for their best interests, and NOT your own, the respect level this builds toward you is immeasurable. As this respect level grows, and they come to understand your concern about them achieving success in their respective roles, they will give you 110% of their abilities each and every day. They will strive to perform their best for you and the team. This leads to "Absolute Teamwork," the kind that lifts every member of the team to new levels of opportunity and advancement—the kind that leaves a lasting impression on every member!

TAKING TRULY CARING TO THE NTH DEGREE

Here's a textbook example on the other side of the spectrum, demonstrating how to be a true, dedicated leader. I'm about to show you how to take the "showing you truly care" philosophy to the nth degree.

I mentioned Ron earlier. He was one hell of a mass-grading fore-man. His skills and abilities at moving dirt were unparalleled. He was a master earthmover, the Beethoven of mass excavation, conducting the symphony orchestra of the scraper spread equipment and making beautiful music with them all day long.

This analogy is more fitting than you know. In reality, before he found his home with us dirt movers, he'd gone to college to pursue his love of classical music. Ron wanted to someday become a professional symphony pianist, but he quickly learned making a living in that industry was very difficult.

Ron started working in the summer months on construction sites with his dad and found a new love—the "art of earthmoving." He fell in love with the grind, the thrill of moving mountains, and the passion of being a builder. The pay was pretty damned good, too.

He started his illustrious career as an oiler or, in technical terms, a lubrication engineer. Ron soon found he had a natural talent for running heavy equipment and moved into heavy civil construction full-time. The rest is history.

As he pursued his destiny as a leader in the mass grading world, he became a highly competent push Cat operator. If you understand scraper operations utilizing push Cats to assist the scrapers in getting loaded, you will sincerely appreciate what is coming.

If you don't have a heavy civil mass grading background, this will be a lesson on one of the many different applications of earthmoving. Most push Cats are Caterpillar D10 Dozers, fitted with special dozer adapters specifically made for pushing scrapers. They are also fitted with what is called a push block in the rear of the dozer. In my mass grading world, two D10 push Cats were utilized in tandem as one team, linking up in perfect unison to PUSH a scraper to get loaded. The front push Cat would move in almost seamlessly, tag the rear push block of the scraper in front of him, and at nearly the exact same instant, the rear push Cat would then link up with the push block on the front push Cat; together, they would push the scraper to get a load of earth.

These push Cat operators were experts in this earthmoving function and could transfer from one scraper to another in seconds, pushing load after load all day long. Seconds were everything in this environment. The faster the push Cats could cycle from one scraper to the next in line, the faster the dirt moved. It is an awesome and spectacular site to see.

The push Cat operators run the cut and direct the scrapers all day with a litany of hand signals, maintaining coordination and organization at the highest productivity levels. Ron could make a push Cat sing like a symphony pianist playing the keys of a grand piano.

> *At this time, I had no idea that Ron was a highly accomplished piano player. Yet I would marvel at how he could orchestrate a scraper cut, keeping everything moving in close to perfect symmetry.*

Later in Ron's career, as a grading foreman, I would learn of his symphony pianist abilities. Then, it all made sense. I wasn't surprised he could supervise a scraper spread like a master conductor leading a symphony orchestra. Ron is retired now and once more pursuing his musical genius, playing that grand piano of his, and I am sure, happily reliving his mass grading days.

But when it came to taking care of his people, there was no other like Ron. He set the example of "showing you truly care." He was the foreman and first to work every morning where he gave 110% of himself to get his crew organized and set up for the shift's success. He was first in line to ensure every crew member had their needs accounted for. He gave breaks to his crew members throughout the day and would run their machines when they hit the "blue room," more commonly known as the on-site portable toilet. He would relieve them if they had to make a phone call during the shift to take care of a family issue. At lunchtime, he was always the LAST to eat and made sure his crewmembers were all taken care of. Ron consistently carried cold water for his crew, and I would see him handing out bottles all day long during the extreme heat of the long Northern California summers.

Ron worked his heart out for his crew, day in and day out. He never once complained about all the extra effort he gave. Not only was he the first to arrive; he was always the last to leave at the end of the shift, and he would give employees rides home if they were having car issues. He tirelessly worked with new hires, getting them accustomed to the crew and the project, and he helped train younger operators on whatever machine they were learning to run. The level of admiration, respect, and loyalty he got from his crew was incredible. Everyone always knew Ron had their back.

Before I continue, let's make one thing perfectly clear. Ron was a taskmaster and hard driver. His expectations on performance and productivity were CRYSTAL CLEAR! He would expect nothing less than precision, Absolute Teamwork, and continuous striving for improvement. Achieving excellence in earthmoving was always his utmost desire.

Despite that, everyone knew, without a doubt, that he cradled his crew in his arms like a new father caring for his newborn baby.

Then, one day, Ron took this care a little too far, and he learned a good lesson that also taught us a lesson.

It was the middle of July; the temps had been averaging 100-plus degrees for what seemed like weeks. With no end to the hot weather, every precaution was taken to keep the crews hydrated and safe. Ron, of course, was the leader of the pack in this particular situation. He made sure that the team had cold water to drink at all times, and he made double sure they were *actually* drinking it. He set up shade canopies before lunch, so the crews could rest and eat lunch and be protected for a bit from the scorching mid-day heat. He gave all the grade setters breaks so they could sit for a few minutes, drink water, and get some much-needed respite from the all-encompassing heat.

It was about 4:00 p.m., and I decided to make my rounds and see how all the operations were going. I was coming back from one of the major excavations performed by the mighty 657 Scrapers when I noticed Ron walking back to his company truck. He was staggering a bit, and I pulled up next to him and exclaimed, "Hey, you ol' dirt stiff, what it is? How's the day treating you?" Ron turned to look at me, and I knew immediately something was wrong. His eyes were foggy, and he was flustered. He tried to answer me, but his words were all garbled. Yes, something was wrong! I also noticed he wasn't sweating. Danger signals flared in my gut.

I leaped out of my truck, grabbed Ron, guided him to the passenger door, opened it quickly, and set him in the seat. I closed the door, cranked up the AC, and made him drink a bottle of water. I grabbed a towel from the back seat, drenched it in cold water, and placed it around his neck. All of this took less than a couple of minutes. After some time, Ron leaned his head back on the seat and mumbled, "Hey, Wolfpack, not feeling too good." I answered back softly, "Covey Leader, I think you have heat exhaustion. Just rest and don't talk. I am taking you to the office now!"

I hit the haul road in overdrive and rushed him to the office, calling for help on the way. When I got there, I was met by damn near the entire office staff. Ron was down, and the whole team was standing in line to help him. The outpouring of love and concern was mind-boggling. We got Ron in the office, set him up by the air conditioner, and covered his head with a wet, cool cloth. After a few minutes, he slowly came around and became coherent. You could see the hurt in his eyes.

Ron had been so concerned about his team in the field that he didn't even take a second to be concerned about himself. He looked up at me, blinked, and said, "How's the crew doing?" With a big smile, I said, "Hey, bro, how are *you* doing? For shit's sake, my brother, you have heat exhaustion! Were you not drinking water all day!? What the hell?!"

Ron sighed, "I guess I got so caught up in taking care of everyone else I forgot to take care of myself. I am so sorry."

"Don't be sorry," I said. "We are all just glad you are going to be okay. You scared the shit out of me!"

Ron let loose with a half-hearted laugh, "I think I may have scared myself a bit! I won't do that again."

The office team anxiously looked on through this entire conversation. There was not a dry eye in the place. We kept a close watch on Ron until he felt better, then he asked to go home and get some rest.

When Ron got to work the next morning, he waved me over to his truck. He had made a sign for himself and taped it to the dashboard. It read, "DRINK WATER ALL DAY. TAKE CARE OF YOUR CREW, AND TAKE CARE OF YOURSELF!" Textbook Ron . . . even after this harrowing experience, he was still putting his team first.

The care he gave his team came straight from his heart, and his desire for all his crew members to succeed and become the best of the best at their particular roles was well-known.

I learned from Ron the true power that comes from treating your people with the highest levels of respect and admiration.

The dynamic results of what a team would do for you were directly correlated to their continual striving for higher performance levels. They performed this way because they knew, without question, that their leader had their best interests in mind—that it was always about them.

That was a life-changing lesson for me. I learned in doing the work to, most importantly, love doing the work to show your team that you truly care about them. This is the epitome of putting into practice one of the essential elements that leads to learning and understanding "What Makes Your Team Tick!"

As I got the blessed opportunity over and over again to train field personnel and members of my office teams, I brought with me this level of concern for each and every individual. No matter what they were learning, the problems they were facing on the job, or their mistakes, I treated them with the utmost levels of dignity, honor, and respect. I gave my all, day in and day out, to help them to succeed. I trained myself to administer the highest levels of patience I could muster when their level of understanding was not quite where I wanted it to be.

As I, like Ron had done, cradled them in my arms like a proud father holding a baby, I came to learn and experience the satisfaction of watching team members improve, grow, and advance in their careers. Showing them that you truly care leads to incredible achievements. Showing them that you truly care and seeing that recognition in their eyes is worth way more than just getting ahead. It's a priceless feeling. I discovered that the drive to help others succeed is all that matters.

Taking the time to develop your people and always putting their needs first is the beginning of showing them you truly care.

A leader is last. Your people always come first!

CHAPTER 13

TRAINING YOUR TEAM— "LEARNING TO TEACH"

"The only thing worse than training your employees and having them leave is not training them and having them stay."
—Henry Ford

Training. In my opinion, it's a frivolous word, yet it's the perfect definition for many construction companies' trainings.

Now, I may get myself in a little trouble here, but if we are really honest with ourselves, and if you or your company have conducted training for your craft or staff personnel, just how effective has that been?

How effective have you been as a trainer or teacher?

Have you been frivolous?

I am not an English teacher, and this is not a lesson in language and definitions. But when I get stuck on a word to describe my thoughts, I go to Mr. Webster.

According to *Webster's Dictionary*, the definition of frivolous means "of little weight or importance" or "lacking in seriousness."[5] I have witnessed a substantial amount of frivolous training, not only in my career but with the clients I have had the opportunity to work for.

Why?

Let me first say that I know training is not easy. It takes time, effort, commitment, and patience, but most importantly, it takes fortitude. Another *Webster* word that can apply to the construction training experience is "fortitude." This means "the strength of mind that enables a person to endure pain or hardship."[6] Thanks, Mr. Webster!

Basically, training can be a real pain in the ass.

That is why many shy away from it. It takes WORK! It takes PAIN! It takes HARDSHIP! It takes all of the above. But when training is done right, and the trainee learns and improves, all the difficulties go away like the snow in the springtime. The preconceived notion of difficulty disappears.

The trainee becomes proficient. Their skill levels and abilities improve. They continue to grow and perform at a higher level, and their overall contribution to the team expands to become huge and empowering. The trainer, in return, receives a level of gratification and fulfillment that *Webster* cannot define—a feeling of accomplishment so strong it cannot be measured. Knowing that you have positively impacted a person for the rest of their life is an indescribably awesome feeling. As a trainer, you have now become a mentor, and when you educate correctly, you will be remembered by the trainee you so

---

5   "Frivolous Definition & Meaning." Merriam-Webster. Accessed November 19, 2024. https://www.merriam-webster.com/dictionary/frivolous.

6   "Fortitude Definition & Meaning." Merriam-Webster. Accessed November 19, 2024. https://www.merriam-webster.com/dictionary/fortitude.

positively impacted forever! It's pretty heavy stuff. Mind-blowing, in fact.

THE RUBBER AND THE ROAD

The rubber meets the road in training when you learn how to teach. Before you can train anyone, you have to learn how you will proceed with imparting your knowledge, experience, and education. You must teach in a way that is easy to understand and comprehend. Of course, you have to be fairly proficient in what exactly you are trying to teach.

> *Let me be clear. Training and teaching are very different in my book. Plenty of my supposed trainers haven't taught me anything.*

Thankfully, the majority of my mentors who have actually taught me have changed my life significantly and enhanced my career substantially. A select few of them continue to do so to this day.

That's the positive side of mindful teaching.

What happens when we do not train or make any effort to grow the people we are working with?

THE REVOLVING DOOR

Many companies wonder why they cannot keep their people. They ask the same questions over and over: "Why are our key people leaving? What are we missing? What are we doing wrong?"

I strongly believe it all comes down to the level of training and teaching individuals receive. But it goes way deeper than that. It centers around the pure passion for and the commitment to teach in such a way that you help people to learn. You need to really care about your mentees' or trainees' overall improvement. Show them that you truly give a damn about helping them to be super successful. Show them that you believe in their ability to grow and become more. Most of all, make them truly feel that they are part of something special—that they are honestly needed.

As they improve their skills and abilities, they are and will become crucial and integral components and contributors to the overall success of the team.

It all starts with learning to learn to teach.

Let's check out a prime example of this basic concept.

MAKE IT HAPPEN

When I first started my business, one of my clients hired me to train a key foreman on The Art of Being a Leader.

This key foreman was a great supervisor. Now, there is a distinct difference between being a supervisor and a leader. This particular foreman, let's call him Carl, worked hard and was very knowledgeable. His crews were always productive, and he was a key player you could count on to get difficult projects done in the field.

But was he a leader of his team? NOT AT ALL! My mission was to help him become a Leader. He had a long way to go.

I happened to be working with him one day when a new laborer was assigned to Carl's crew. This kid was young; I guessed him at 19-20 years old. He was as green as the grass on a well-manicured golf course.

Carl's crews were working on a variety of operations, one of them backfilling a small ditch that had been recently excavated to hold erosion-control blanket on a steep slope. The materials from the ditch were piled up neatly in a windrow on the opposite side of the ditch. Carl instructed the new laborer to begin backfilling the ditch.

I looked on in amusement as the whole scenario played out before me. Carl instructed the laborer, Jeff, to grab a shovel from the back of his work truck and start filling up the ditch. Jeff had no idea about these instructions. So, he grabbed a round-point shovel (likely the first shovel he saw in the back of the truck) and began dragging the pile of dirt into the ditch. He was straddling the ditch and dragging the end of the round point shovel through the pile of dirt, pulling the loose dirt toward himself into the open ditch, trying to secure and bury the erosion-control blanket.

I watched with round eyes, knowing full well Jeff had no idea what he was doing. I closed my eyes and reminisced again about "Hank," my long-time close friend and colleague's voice saying, "He is screwed up like a homemade radio."

I felt sorry for this kid. About this time, here came Carl. He was very unhappy and yelled at Jeff, "What in the world are you doing? Haven't you ever backfilled a ditch before? Oh my God! Don't they teach you guys anything at the Laborers Training Center?"

Carl strode up to me, hell-bent for leather, and exclaimed, "See what I have to put up with. I am going to fire this worthless kid! He doesn't know shit! He can't even run a shovel."

Of course, Jeff heard all this. He hung his head in disbelief and embarrassment, a sad look on his face. The rest of the crew was silent. They had all witnessed Carl's outbursts before.

I felt this was an opportune time for me to teach Carl a lesson on how to teach. I walked up to him and quietly but firmly said, "Carl, give me five minutes with this kid. Watch exactly what I do. Don't say a word. Just stand here and watch and learn."

Carl grudgingly agreed, and I walked up to Jeff, looked him directly in the eye, and asked, "Jeff, have you ever used a shovel before?" His response: "Hell no, there ain't no shovels where I come from. I just got into the Laborers Union as an apprentice, and I have never even seen a damn shovel. This is bullshit!"

I calmly replied, "Well, Jeff, today is your lucky day. Not only am I going to show you and teach you what a shovel is, I am going to teach you how to use it correctly and efficiently. You up for that?"

"Hell yes," Jeff replied. "I ain't afraid of hard work. I just need to know how to do it."

"Perfect," I boomed. "Then let's get to it."

I took Jeff by the shoulders and said, "First of all, young man, you have the wrong shovel for the job. A round-point shovel is made for digging. This operation requires a flat-head shovel."

I went around to the back of Carl's truck and pulled out a flat-head shovel. I held the shovel out in front of me, and Jeff took it as I explained, "Now, Jeff, this is a flat-head shovel. It has specific applications, and this is one of them." I walked Jeff over to the ditch that was to be backfilled and stood on the same side of the stockpiled dirt.

"Okay, Jeff," I smiled, "the trick here is to let the shovel do the work. Slide the flat head of the shovel on the ground, under the windrow of dirt, and shove the dirt into the open trench. When the flat head of the shovel crosses the open trench, quickly pull back on it and let the dirt fall right into the trench. Let the shovel do the work. Keep the smooth, flat part of the shovel on the surface of the ground and take a little at a time, filling the flat head of the shovel, then letting the dirt fall into the open hole of the ditch."

I demonstrated the technique to him several times. Jeff was shocked and couldn't believe how easy it was—that it took such little effort. He liked that the method was fast.

I continued: "Now, Jeff, hold the shovel just like I showed you and give it a try." Jeff took the shovel and went to work.

He mastered the technique in all but a few seconds, and off he went. The grin on his face said it all. "I got this down!" Jeff cried out. "Get out of my way, and I'll backfill this whole son-of-a-bitch faster than anyone else here can."

I let out a big ol' laugh and yelled back, "Let's see what you got, young man!"

When I glanced over at Carl, the expression on his face was utter astonishment. He looked like he'd just won the winning lottery ticket. I walked over to him with a grin. He asked, "How the hell did you do that?"

I leaned forward and softly whispered, "Carl, you have to learn how to teach. Simple as that. You were ready to write that kid off, fire him on the spot, and send him back to the Union Hall. Look at him now!"

We both turned and stood there, watching Jeff work away.

Jeff was greased lightning. He had that flat-head shovel singing a tune. He moved down the ditch, backfilling the open trench like a well-oiled machine. In less than five minutes, he had covered over 40 feet. His technique was close to perfect. He moved with precision, and it was a beautiful sight to behold.

I felt the same chill run down my back I had felt many times before. It was the warm afterglow of knowing that I had just significantly impacted a young man's life over such a minor training scenario. It's a sensation I never get tired of. This was a kid who may have never been given a second chance before. The confidence Jeff gained in that short training session oozed out of him. He went on to attack the ditch with gusto, a gleam in his eyes, a smile playing on his face.

Carl gazed at me through strained eyes. Tears welled up, but I knew there was no way he would let them flow. He gained control of himself then spoke in a near whisper, his voice heavy with emotion, "I suck as a foreman. I was ready to write that kid off. Look at him now. What the hell is wrong with me?"

I put my hand on his shoulder and said, "Carl, look at me." By then, he was staring at the ground as if something interesting lay there. He lifted his head and gave me a blank stare. "Look, Carl," I soothed, "being able to train your people takes effort. It takes commitment. It takes patience. It takes fortitude. You are a good foreman. You just have to learn how to teach. You have so much knowledge and experience to share with your team. You are an expert in this field. You can teach any and all these crew members everything you know. Look at Jeff go. Just look at him! He will have that entire 300 lineal feet of trench backfilled in the next couple of hours, and then he will be looking for more! I will help you learn how to teach." Now, I had a big cat-that-swallowed-the-canary grin on my face.

"You will train your crewmembers, Carl, and I promise you that you will develop a team that will move mountains for you. That, Carl, is the secret. It's what makes a supervisor a LEADER, and once you master this whole concept of training and teaching, you will be unstoppable. There will be nothing your team will not do for you! They will run through brick walls for you!" (I call this "The Brick Wall Syndrome," and one of the key ingredients to achieve it is training!)

Without a word, Carl strode off toward Jeff. I stood in awe, watching Carl talking to Jeff as huge smiles appeared on both of their faces. I felt that same chill as Carl shook Jeff's hand and patted him on the shoulder.

When Carl walked back toward me, I knew he was a changed man. He had witnessed the absolute power of teaching and training, and most importantly, he had cared enough to help someone learn something new. Carl approached me and burst out, "Damn, that feels good! Oh, and Jeff just told me I better watch out. He is going to be a foreman soon! He wants to be a foreman. Can you friggin' believe that?!"

I let out a hearty laugh, "Oh yes, I certainly can!"

Carl grasped my hand tightly. "Okay, Morelock Motivational, let's get with it. I have a lot to learn about teaching . . . and I like it!"

That little voice in my head whispered softly but convincingly, *well, here we go again.*

As I walked away with Carl, hand on his shoulder, a warm rush flooded over me. I knew Carl would be a great leader.

CHAPTER 14

YOU ARE NEVER DONE LEARNING OR TEACHING

"Intellectual growth should begin at birth and cease only at death."
—Albert Einstein

Training your team never ends. It is a virtual constant, like the turning of the planets as they orbit the sun, like the turning of the tides in the ocean. Training is always moving, never stopping. As training takes root and learning how to teach pays its dividends, momentum increases.

It is similar to a NASA Saturn V rocket propelling an Apollo spacecraft into outer space. There is a brief lull in the initial ascent of the rocket and the attached spacecraft. When the engines first ignite, the rocket almost hovers in place for a moment. As compression builds, the rocket accelerates off the launch pad—slowly at first; then, as the engines fire off and go into full burn, the compounding forces of the fully ignited engines propel the rocket upward, and acceleration increases dramatically. The rocket pushes the spacecraft upward at incredible speeds, out of the Earth's atmosphere to its desired destination, into the limitless reaches of outer space.

Good training creates the same team reaction as the launch of the Saturn V rocket.

The initial process takes time; there is a brief slowdown in forward momentum as the training occurs. Then, almost magically, as skill levels and abilities improve from the training, the team's performance improves. The team accelerates forward, becoming better and better.

Soon, through increased training and a focus on Continuous Improvement, the team becomes a force all its own, growing and empowering itself to accomplish what was once considered unachievable.

Training spans the gamut and can be as simple as instructing someone how to use a shovel to demonstrating to a mass grading fleet how to most efficiently move nine million cubic yards of earth.

Let's take a look at that example.

MOVING THE EARTH . . . QUICKLY

The company I was working for at the time had won the bid to build a subdivision development in the foothills above Dublin, California. The project was enormous and included a tremendous amount of mass excavation and grading and a plethora of wet utility underground installation.

The I-580 Freeway bordered one entire side of the project. It was going to be a very tough project to build and required experienced craft personnel. This was no place for beginners or unskilled operators and laborers.

During this time in Northern California's history, the housing market and pretty much every other type of construction infrastructure work was booming. Building was going on everywhere, and it was a beautiful thing.

It was my first major project as a project manager, and I was so excited to get started. We put together a solid management team, including the "best of the best" craft field supervisors. The problem was, due to the glut of work going on all over Northern California, the pool of highly skilled, seasoned, experienced craft workers was hard to come by.

Our initial start was not very impressive. The craft supervisors and I began to get worried.

Not only was the project difficult to build, but the work was also dangerous. Heavy equipment operators—including scraper, dozer, excavator, loader, blade, and compactor operators—had to run the earthmoving equipment required. Laborers had to be skilled pipe layers with experience laying pipe in steep terrain. Every single person on the job had to be highly skilled. Unfortunately, there just were not enough people with that needed skillset to go around.

Driving into the job early one morning, I was hit with the realization that the only way we were going to make this happen was to train like we had never trained before. I thought back to all the companies I had worked for in the past. I remembered all my great mentors. They had mastered the technique of learning how to teach. I was a living, breathing byproduct of their knowledge and ability to teach.

The majority of the craft supervisors on the project were cut from the same cloth. Knowing this, I gathered them all up in the office that early morning and around the conference table and stated, "Ladies and gentlemen, we are going to be successful. Come hell or high water, we are going to win, and we are going to bring this project to the finish line ahead of schedule *and* under budget. Most importantly, and above all else, no one is going to get hurt. NO ONE! So, how are we going to accomplish this feat?"

The blank stares coming back at me caused a brief moment of anxiety and hesitation. "Glad you asked," I went on. "We are going to embark on full-on training mode. Now, gather around and let me share my idea. Feel free to chime in with your thoughts and ideas. But training is what we are going to do, and training is what will get us there! Are you with me?!"

To give you a sense of the mood in the room and the reception of my message, let me share that the cars and trucks passing by a quarter-mile below on I-580 could have heard the roar from the team. The rallying cry "Let's Do This!" became the mantra. "MAKE IT HAPPEN" was the goal.

My initial idea was to utilize the NFL's playbook. My question to the team was, "Why do NFL teams spend the first part of the week, before their next Sunday game, watching videos of their previous game?"

This crew knew the answer and hollered it back, "They watch videos to learn and improve in their specific roles!"

"EXACTLY," I shouted. "And now, we are going to embark on the same proven approach. We will take video daily of the ongoing operations. ALL OF THEM."

Supervisors in the field would record both the operators and laborers performing their work perfectly at the various ongoing operations. Then, they would take video of the operators and laborers who appeared challenged and needed to improve their skills. We would bring the team of operators and laborers into the office for lunch every day, and we would all watch and critique the videos together so the team members could see themselves in action and learn where they were or were not proficient in their operations.

The team loved it, and we had a mission.

It was time to ignite the engines of the Saturn V rocket.

VIDEO REVIEW

I will never forget our first video review lunch with the craft teams. We kept it under wraps so everyone would want to participate. The craft teams were seated around the tables in the conference room, hot pizza and cold soda at the ready for this pack of wolves about to dive into a fresh moose carcass! I strode into the room, wearing my favorite New England Patriot's Tom Brady jersey, and exclaimed, "Ladies and Gentlemen, WELCOME TO THE NFL!" The roar of laughter calmed down the room.

I went on to explain what we were doing and why and was already getting buy-in—I could see by the rapt expression on people's faces. The overall results of that buy-in remained to be seen, but at least we were there, exploring how we were really doing and our precise mechanisms. We sat there for one hour and watched video after video.

> All the craft supervisors and I gave play-by-play explanations. We critiqued, commented, and used our experience and expertise to help the craft employees learn and improve.

Soon, to my astonishment, the more experienced—the highly skilled operators—were taking turns giving advice and sharing "how-to" explanations. The craft employees who were struggling listened intently and asked question after question, for which there was always a definitive answer on technique and know-how. No one was ever made to feel less than or a subordinate. Everyone was treated with respect. The only goal was to help every member of the team get better and become all they could be!

Everyone absolutely loved the video training sessions. To my greatest surprise, an offshoot component of these sessions that I did not anticipate was that both the craft and staff supervisors got a lesson in the art of learning to teach. It was incredible.

We continued these video training sessions a few times a week over the next six months.

Where we'd once experienced a remaking of the movie *The Bad News Bears* at the beginning of this project, we were now becoming a recreation of the movie *Miracle on Ice*. Our challenges paralleled those overcome by the 1976 USA Olympic Hockey Team in defeating the invincible Russian team to win the Gold Medal. It was a feat that had never been accomplished before. And we were on the same track.

I was quickly learning the power of effective training, the results of showing individuals that you truly cared about their growth and advancement of their skills and abilities, and the impact their growth and learning had on the performance and success of the team. The camaraderie that grew on the project, the attitude of helping each other be the best we could be, and the accomplishments we achieved together were overwhelming.

Craft supervisors who had not yet learned how to become field leaders quickly became leaders that even Vince Lombardi and General George S. Patton would have been proud of. I continued my own education on learning how to teach. The effects I experienced and that I saw reflected in every member of the team were phenomenal. The best part was that we *did* complete a very successful project, and no one had a scratch on them!

Near the end of the project, as we were building the most difficult mountainside fill that would be the last major assault for the mass grading portion of the job, I was overwhelmed with how far this team had come. As we reached the top of the fill, late one fall afternoon, with 657 Scrapers struggling to climb the steep haul roads, placing fill with the help of support dozers on the side of this mountain, I saw a vision in my mind of Edmund Hillary, his sherpa, Tenzing Norgay and the team of mountain climbers making the first successful ascent of Mt. Everest. I reflected on how they overcame what seemed like insurmountable odds to successfully make it to the top of one of the highest mountains on Earth.

Of course, I would never take anything away from this remarkable achievement, and I can only imagine Edmund Hillary's thrill as he planted the British flag atop this majestic peak. But our team of builders had also overcome almost impossible odds and could now finish their last massive undertaking on their own mountain atop the foothills of Northern California.

I rushed back to the office, grabbed an American flag that we flew on all the national holidays, and quickly called team members to share my vision with them. Within the next hour, all the craft, staff, and maintenance personnel—the entire project field management team—met up at the top of that mountain. As the last scraper load was dumped and the last dozer push of fill material to finish off the slope was pushed into place, we all gathered around that American flag.

Together, as a team, we placed that flag atop that mountain fill in honor of all the intense training and remarkable improvement of the team members who had worked tirelessly to bring the project to the finish line—from the "Let's Do This" to the "MAKE IT HAPPEN." We all stood there motionless for what seemed like an eternity, watching the flag blow beautifully in the wind, knowing we were all part of something very, very special.

I walked off from the group and stood there alone, watching my team bask in the glory of what they had all achieved, a sense of immense pride welling up inside me.

I sensed a loving presence surrounding me. It was as if I could feel Herman Hall and Bob Daniels, two of my greatest mentors from many years ago, standing right there beside me.

I do believe that as I continue to learn and teach, my long-departed mentors still talk to me. I let them guide me at every opportunity.

A gentle breeze brushed across my sweat-stained face. As I quietly walked away, I heard their voices softly whisper, "Awesome team, Lonnie. Awesome job."

CHAPTER 15

THE PURSUIT OF CONTINUOUS IMPROVEMENT

"An 'overwhelming desire to improve' is the key ingredient in the recipe for success. A lack of this key ingredient leads to substandard performance and eventual failure."
—Lonnie S. Morelock, 2011

Before we dive into the concept of Continuous Improvement, let's define the phrase. I looked up "Continuous" and "Improvement" in *Webster's Dictionary* online; the definition of these two words combined together creates my own definition, which I believe should be: "Continuous Improvement: Marked by an uninterrupted extension in space, time, or sequence coupled with the act or process of improving, enhancing value and/or excellence." We *want* to find excellence in everything. We *don't want* to be satisfied with just being good.

Think deeply about what you have just read. "An uninterrupted extension in space . . . [or] time." That means Continuous Improvement (whatever it is) never stops, NEVER!

The overall thought process means the state of being improved, all while enhancing the value and excellence of an entire entity. It is ongoing. Never-ending. For infinity. It is POWERFUL! INTENSE! POTENT!

I sometimes believe I have lived my entire life in a state of Continuous Improvement. I always strive to be better and look for every way to get just a little bit more polished and refined. I pick apart every opportunity to advance my talents, skills, and abilities and am relentlessly driven to be the absolute best I can be. From the time I first sat down in a 657 Scraper to this very day as a leadership development consultant, one thought has repeatedly gone through my head: "How do I get better? How can I improve?"

The first old-timer 657 hands I worked with were masters in the trade. They could do things with their scrapers that were out of this world. Barry and Lou were two perfect examples of this statement. They were a precision team. They thought and moved like one piece of earthmoving machinery.

> *I would watch them in absolute awe of their skills, talents, and abilities throughout the day. Had there been a show back then like Dancing with the Stars, Barry and Lou would have been their premier performers.*

I asked them so many questions so often I was sure they would get sick and tired of me. But they never did. They shared everything they knew and were happy to do it. I treated them with the utmost respect and honor at all times. They were like superstar professional football players. The best of the best! The "Top Guns" of scraper operators. I often asked them how they got so damn good—how they made what they did look so effortless, painless, and so uncommonly graceful.

Their response was always the same. "Lonnie, we are always looking at ways to improve. Always trying to figure out what more these awesome machines can do. We're exploring new methods and techniques. Asking, what more can we learn? We are never satisfied."

The entire crew and I watched them once dive off what must have seemed like a 1,000-foot beaver slide, following each other in perfect sequence. They push-pulled over the almost-vertical edge, starting a new cut from the top of one of the many mountains being moved to the dam fill waiting for them at the bottom of the gorge. We were working in the foothills east of Healdsburg, California, on Warm Springs Dam, now Lake Sonoma—the first project I'd ever worked on. As a new operating engineer, it was spectacular.

I will never forget that day! D10 Dozers prepped the cut for eons. All the scraper hands watched day after day as the dozers pushed material off the precipice, forming the straight up-and-down beaver slide leading to the valley floor.

We all wondered how in the hell any scraper could ever go off that. It was menacing, frightening, almost unimaginable. I thought, *oh hell no! I am not going off of that. Sorry, not interested*, as my knees shook uncontrollably. I suspect the rest of the crew felt the same way.

> *We all knew it was dangerous, and the question was, were the machines made for such an operation? We weren't sure.*

But when Barry and Lou bailed off that cut, gliding down the beaver slide effortlessly, like a pro ice skater performing a quadruple axle, it was an awesome sight to see. The crew roared in acknowledgment of their skill and daring. "Go get 'em, boys," was the battle cry. "Give 'em hell, Barry," and "Kick some ass, Lou!" rang out in the hills, the screams and hollers continuing for eternity. When Barry and Lou reached the bottom, they made a graceful, sweeping turn following the newly bladed haul road, set up together in perfect symmetry, and dumped their loads in the fill area.

Roars from the crew rang out again!

At that very moment, I came to understand where Continuous Improvement could take you and where the thoughts and actions of improving and chasing excellence through an uninterrupted extension in time could lead you.

On that day, I knew in my heart, soul, and mind that striving for Continuous Improvement was, and still is, THE ONLY WAY TO LIVE!

CONTINUOUS IMPROVEMENT–TAKE TWO

My next major lesson in the value and mindset of Continuous Improvement could not have come at a more opportune time.

I was a job superintendent on one of my first mass grading projects. This job consisted of a mix of 657 Scrapers, 651 Scrapers, and Cat D400 articulating trucks. At this point of my Continuous Improvement epiphany, the project was a complete shit show. We were basically losing our ass on a daily basis!

The job entailed the excavation of a large, deep drainage channel; we had to cut/fill pads for a future housing development and an 18-hole golf course.

While it was rough, it was a dirt mover's dream. Unfortunately, this dream quickly turned into a nightmare as we struggled with water and mud in the drainage channel. The majority of the cuts in the earthmoving vernacular were pure "potato dirt." But the material being excavated from the future drainage channel was extremely wet, making the fills we were building difficult to dry out. We were continuously fighting to get compaction with the over-saturated material. This difficulty with the wet, muddy material was then compounded by dozer crews spending way too much time to finish the future house pads to the required specifications of +/- one-tenth of a foot. The job was upside down, and I was experiencing my first gut-wrenching punch of having a real loser on my hands.

The field supervisors were frustrated, the equipment operators were frustrated, and my senior manager . . . well, let's just say he was a bit concerned, to put it mildly. I was having such a hard time understanding what was actually wrong since I was so new. *How can this be happening? We have the best damn earthmoving team in the business. What are we missing? What Am I Missing?* I didn't know it then, but this phrase would later become a focal backbone of my future training program: "WHAT AM I MISSING?!"

A large stockpile of material from the project was strategically located near the dead center of the job. It was one of my favorite project lookouts and offered great visibility to all that was going on below. I was sitting up there early one morning, watching the continuing carnage, my stomach churning with thoughts of impending financial disaster, when an idea popped into my head. It all wrapped around the phrase, "What Am I Missing?"

I radioed to my key foreman, several of our lead grade setters, and my young project engineer and beckoned them to meet me up on the stockpile. I figured, *what the hell? I might as well include everyone in this inevitable sinking of the ship*.

> *We all gathered together and stood at the edge of the stockpile, staring down at the scene below.*

I looked at every one of them and asked the group, "Guys, what are we missing? What Am I Missing? We have some of the best earthmoving minds and talent in the business as well as this young engineer who is pretty damned smart. We are trying to focus on getting better each day, but that is not working. We all know we are in trouble, so let's put our brains to work and figure this friggin' mess out. How do we fix it?! What methods of improvement are we not seeing!?"

Ron and Dave, our mass-grading WWF championship tag team, both exclaimed at damn near the same time. "Lonnie, we have looked at this mess 10 ways to Sunday, and we can't figure it out!" Jeff, one of our awesome grade setters, quietly added, "There are just too many variables that we can't seem to control."

I always loved the way Jeff talked—very calm and comforting—a contrast to how I felt at that very moment. I quickly asked Pete, our young engineer, to share his thoughts. Pete looked back at me, a smart-engineer grin on his face, and replied, "I am thinking."

Now, that was a pretty good answer. I looked at the entire team and clapped my hands together. "That is just what we need to do, team! We need to think more. We need to look at every single opportunity to improve on what we are doing. There has to be a way!"

Pete had given me a new direction to go, and I had to marinate on that for a minute. I wanted the team to do this, too, so I said, "Okay. Here is what we are going to do. We are all going to sit up here on this perfect overlook vantage point. Absolutely no talking, just sitting and looking and analyzing. We are going to sit up here until Hell freezes over if that is what it takes, and until we figure out what our next move is. Now, let's plop our asses down on this stockpile and start mind-bending on what we are looking at."

With that, we sat in silence, each of us intently focusing on the activity below. Not a word was spoken. It was almost as if time stood still, and we were in a slow-motion movie. I could feel the wheels turning in my team's brains. I wondered what the crews below must have been thinking, craning their necks up at all of us hunkered there on the edge of the stockpile, no one moving, just sitting and staring. Maybe they thought we had all lost our minds and that the hot summer sun had fried our brains.

To this day, I do not remember who spoke first, but the proverbial dam broke, and the problem-solving water started flowing out. Slowly at first, but then like a massive wave generated from a dam failure, rushing over all of us.

"Look," Dave exclaimed. "This job is shaped like a big rectangular box, but really, it's just one big circle."

Ron's eyes snapped open. He could see the picture Dave was painting, and he quickly added, "Hell yes, there are five separate cuts and fills. They are all linked together." The mutual 200-watt light bulb was now going off in everyone's minds, illuminating the way.

"Yes," I screamed, jumping up and shaking with excitement. "This is it. This is what we were missing. You guys are truly on to something! SWEET!"

I walked as I spoke, the words flying out of my mouth, matching the energy of my body, which wouldn't be still.

I punched the air. "We need to set this whole operation up in a precisely controlled sequential manner, working one cut to fill, one after the other, following the actual shape of the job. We need to let the job work with us, not against us!"

BAM! My dad's words of wisdom from long ago rang through my ears. I could hear his voice as clear as day. "Son, remember, if you look at a job long enough, it will talk to you. You have to look and listen. It will show itself to you and tell you what to do."

The hair stood up on my arms. I looked up to Heaven, wondering if I would see his face glowing down on me. A warm energy surrounded me.

Jeff's voice pulled me out of my moment of reflection. "Look, my earthmoving brothers, we can start at one end of the job, cut to fill in each separate location, and keep moving forward, processing and discing the wet material behind us as we go. Using this beautiful summer heat that we love so much, by the time we get to the last cut, fill number five, we will have fill number one compacted and sold, and we can start all over. We will springboard from one cut and fill to the other."

I almost fell over.

My mind immediately went to one of my all-time favorite comedies, *Back to School*, starring Rodney Dangerfield. (If you haven't seen it, it's funny as hell.) In the movie, Rodney volunteers to compete in the college's high diving championship. He goes on to pull off what he calls the "Triple Lindy." In this ingenious move, he utilizes three different diving boards, diving, twisting, and turning from one diving board to the next, and finishing his final dive from the last springboard with an unbelievable inward, inverted twist. He wins the competition! The crowd goes wild!

I screamed so loud; I think the whole project heard me. "We are going to do the Triple Lindy!" Everyone looked at me with questions on their faces, exclaiming in perfect unison. "What the hell is the Triple Lindy?" I started laughing so hard I couldn't control myself. The crew for sure thought I had lost my mind.

I quickly explained, "Look, I can't get into the particulars of what that means right now, but trust me, with all your input, we are going to shake this place up. Let's go put this brilliant idea on the grease board, detail the exact approach, then put 'er into action!"

That is exactly what we did. The plan was truly brilliant. We used everyone's ideas together, weaving each improvement idea into the overall attack plan. Then, we were ready to go. I was guardedly optimistic, but something inside me told me this would be yet another turning point in my career.

That night, I stopped by what was then a Blockbuster Video Store. Back in the day, if you needed a movie to rent, they had it. I rented *Back to School*, then headed home. I couldn't wait to return to the job the following morning. The anticipation was killing me!

The office had a TV with a VHS recorder. Yes, oh yes, that was "back in the day." With his engineering skills and brain, Pete rigged up the TV outside on my truck bed, so the whole crew could see it. Ron and Dave brought out the grease board, and we went through the entire plan with the team. Everyone was on fire! Our strategy looked airtight, and positivity enveloped the crew.

After sharing the plan with the crew, I went into what I did not know would become full-on Morelock Motivational mode. I whipped up the team into a frenzy, focusing on all the new ideas. Then I showed them the part in the movie where Rodney Dangerfield performs the "Triple Lindy." "That," I exclaimed, "is precisely what we are going to do, guys. We are doing the TRIPLE LINDY!"

The team cheered.

You can probably figure out the end of this story. We went on to completely turn this job around, beating the original schedule by a fair margin and destroying the original estimate. The project went from what was tracking to be a dismal loser to one awe-inspiring winner!

As the days proceeded, our plan was flawless. We searched each day for additional methods of improvement. "Continuous Improvement" became the preferred slogan for the job.

We developed an "out-of-the-box" MacGyver method for drying out the wet, muddy material excavated from the drainage channel and fondly nicknamed it "The Plow." The Plow was designed by one of our super Brainy-Smurf master mechanics and was made of welded sheet metal formed into the shape of an over-sized plow, then rigged to fit on a single ripper shank on the back of a D10 Dozer.

The 657 Scrapers spread out the saturated material in a strategic, large, flat area within our work zone. Then, taking advantage of Mother Nature and the 100-plus-degree summer heat, we plowed the material back and forth with the D10 until it was at an optimum moisture level to be placed in the fills.

Doing this allowed us to achieve a double benefit. Not only could we dry out the material quickly and efficiently, but we could also load out the fill-readied material on the 657 Scrapers' return cycle to the ongoing "cut-fill" operations. This technique in the earth-moving world is referred to as the coveted "backhaul," which means setting up scrapers to move material constantly in both directions without ever having an empty load. The "backhauled" material was then placed in the golf course fills, allowing the crews to build both portions of the project at the same time.

The icing on the cake was that this new method accelerated the golf course construction well ahead of schedule.

We fondly referred to our new operational approach as the "Quintuple Lindy," meaning we were using five diving boards in a row and/or five sequential operations simultaneously. I would have loved to watch Rodney Dangerfield attempt that one! Yes, it was a stunning sight to behold.

Following this project's success, I relentlessly focused on the "Continuous Improvement Mindset." No matter what I was up against, whether it was a good or bad situation, I was always "peeling back the onion" to uncover every opportunity to improve. Analyzing every approach, method, technique, procedure, practice, system, and on and on and on to find the "holy grail" of Continuous Improvement was my obsession—still is to this day.

Living by the tenet of Continuous Improvement is all-consuming. It is a search that never ends. But, without a doubt, it leads to the eventual discovery of "What Makes Your Team Tick!" . . . and success always follows close behind.

CHAPTER 16

LIGHTING THE FUSE— STOKING THE FIRE

"Passion is the driving force of successful outcomes. Where passion is lacking, there is no follow-through. But true passion unleashes a tidal wave of energy and focus, which eventually leads to what was once perceived as unachievable results."
—Lonnie S. Morelock, 2009

Passion is a very powerful word that breeds intensity! When I contemplate my passion for history, I can't help but recognize the different levels of passion that have driven so much of human history. The passion to excel. The passion to improve. The passion to invent.

I've always been mystified by the different inventions that were thought of, created, and implemented to improve human life. And there are so many monumental examples.

There's the Wright brothers and their passion for learning how to fly. Look how far we have come from that first flight at Kitty Hawk.

Could these brothers ever have imagined the creation of the Boeing 787 Dreamliner inspired by their first flight?

What about Alexander Graham Bell and his passion to communicate? If he could only see the methods of communication we have now. The smartphone, the internet, etc., all built upon what he started with his invention of the telegraph.

Henry Ford and his passion for developing a different method of travel across the ground led to every car that has ever been driven. The horse was great then as the only known mode of ground transportation, and wagons were efficient, but his passion opened the door to much greater achievements in travel. I am sure he would love to have the opportunity to take a drive in a Shelby Mustang GT Turbo! And I'm sure Carrol Shelby would have gotten along great with O' Henry Ford.

Passion has had a huge influence in shaping my career. My passion to be a dirt mover, like my dad and grandfather before me, bred my overall passion for being a builder. My passion to give speeches and presentations paved the way to my passion for developing people. PASSION IS A DRIVER. It has sat with me as I typed away, writing this book and sharing my passion for leadership development, building superstar construction teams, and the learning process of "What Makes a Team Tick?"

When I first started running a scraper, my passion was to move mountains. What a thrill it was to feel the power of the Cat 657 Scraper with its dual front and rear engines generating 900-plus horsepower underneath me! The incredible volume of "Mother Earth" that could be moved in a shift allowed me to shape the ground into whatever the plans and project called for. I jumped out of bed every morning, racing to the project site to get back on that scraper and enjoy the sheer delight of yet another day of earthmoving magic! As I think about it even today, it sends a shiver through me.

After becoming a grading foreman, my passion shifted to supervising a crew to be the best they could be. I poured into them the passion to be the best earthmovers and the best builders on planet Earth.

This passion continued as my career moved forward. It morphed into a passion to build an earthmoving team that was a formidable force in the heavy construction realm. I quickly learned that as I shared my passion, excitement, and unbridled enthusiasm for the work, this same passion infected my supervisors and crews.

It became a daily challenge to see how good and fast we could be and how to continuously improve to achieve absolute precision. This passion permeated the entire crew and the project team. The result was unflagging remarkable productivity.

We focused on how much dirt we could move in a 10-hour shift and strove to increase the total quantities every day. That focused mindset grew to how much we could accelerate our earthmoving by the minute. Every single minute counted, and there was no wasted effort.

That led to the pursuit of the "almighty second." We grew our knowledge to understand the value of a second. Then, we looked for every opportunity to shave seconds off load, dump, and cycle times.

The desire and lust for more productivity each day grew like a hurricane forming in the Atlantic. Our frenzied energy was equivalent to a spark starting a small fire, and that fire surging into a wild entity, devouring everything in its path. The passion was so magnificent, the thrill of pursuing Continuous Improvement so intense that at the end of each shift, the team was beyond exhausted.

THE POWER OF PASSION

Vince Lombardi, legendary leader and National Football League Coach of the Green Bay Packers, had that same passion. He possessed the drive, dedication to improve, and the innate desire to perform at the highest level. He drove his players and teams with that passion, resulting in an overwhelming success story. He summed it up best with this famous quote, "But I firmly believe that in every man's finest hour, the greatest fulfillment for all he holds dear is when he has worked his heart out for a good cause, then lies down on the field of battle, exhausted but victorious." That quote is the embodiment of passion's definition.

As I grew in my leadership abilities, I realized God had given me the gift of passion. He had given me the gift of igniting excitement and enthusiasm in those around me and the gift of using that passion to bring out the best of others' God-given talents and abilities.

Another favorite quote of mine that explains passion perfectly goes like this:

"People are like sticks of dynamite. The power is on the inside, but nothing happens until the fuse gets lit."
—Mac Anderson

I developed a burning passion to light that fuse in my team, all the while lighting it inside myself daily. Then, I focused on methods and techniques to fan the flame in my team members, from igniting the spark of enthusiasm to building the bonfire toward the pursuit of excellence.

Just writing these words and recalling the great teams of the past I've had the honor to be associated with gets me jittery all over! That is the level of passion a leader must figure out how to extract from their team. This passion, this obsession, is the key ingredient to fully understanding "What Makes Your Team Tick?!"

A leader must look into the eyes and hearts of their team. The team must feel what they are feeling as the leader probes their psyches, personalities, and temperaments to discern their fuse.

As a leader, you must know what sparks your team.

What opens up their desire for achievement?

What opens the door to their fanaticism for improvement?

Once you fully understand that, you can "stoke the fire."

LEADERSHIP IS A CAMPFIRE

The process of imparting your passion to your team is like making a campfire in the woods. First, you'll find some good dry kindling, like dead twigs, grass, etc. Pile it all up carefully, and then light the spark. These are the first key ingredients for finding the emotional drivers for yourself and your team.

Once the spark is lit, a small ember glows. The kindling, the twigs, and the grass will create a tiny flame. When you lean forward and breathe ever so slowly and softly into the flame, poof, the entire bundle will ignite. As you add smaller pieces of wood to the now-growing flame, they will flicker to life, and then you can add larger pieces of wood, strategically placing them where they will get the most exposure to the flames.

Before long, a blaze will develop and feed off the larger pieces of wood. Soon, you can add more and more fuel to the fire. The fire will leap up and become a force all its own, which will envelop the entire campsite in bright light and cozy warmth. What started as a tiny little spark is now a roaring bonfire.

The roaring bonfire is an example of the end result that an individual or team gets from the entire progression mentioned above.

This campfire illustrates how the whole process works when developing and instilling passion within yourself and your team.

The beauty of developing people is that each and every individual has a different fuse or spark. Everyone has a different type of passion or minute detail that sets off a chain reaction within them that then propels them into the desire to grow in their specific talent and ability to become the best they can be.

Finding this "fuse" is the secret sauce.

Developing the fuse, improving it, and putting processes and procedures in place to build upon is the pathway to achievement never before thought possible.

When developing your team, you must use all the tools around you to nurture each individual. On huge mass grading teams, I spent hours helping the foremen develop their talents and earthmoving abilities and the finish foremen develop their expertise in building the finished house pads, cut slopes, fill slopes, and streets. The emphasis was always to aim for speed and accuracy.

The different teams of heavy equipment operators, dozer hands, scraper hands, compactor operators, and blade hands and I all continuously worked to ignite our passion for our craft as we concentrated on being our best. At every opportunity, in every aspect of the art of earthmoving, processes and practices were implemented to improve the team as a whole. All of the above came together to form a mass grading team capable of producing continuous great results. PASSION was always the motivator. PASSION was always the starting point.

WELCOME TO DUBLIN

I was standing on a hillside one day on one of the largest mass grading operations I had ever managed in my career. We were building a large new housing development in the hills above Dublin, California. To make this happen, we had to move the existing mountains.

At one point, the team had strategized for days to develop an "attack plan," allowing for multiple excavation operations. They would work simultaneously, hauling and placing all the excavated material in the same massive fill area. The detailed planning, organization, coordination, and precise choreography it took to implement this operation was staggering. I still have a crystal-clear memory of it, and what an awesome site it was to see.

It was 10:00 a.m. when my key project foreman pulled up in his truck and jumped out to join me on my perch, where I was intently watching all the action below. Ron was a master earthmover. He also just happened to be the son of the master grade setter who had trained me years ago.

> *This was no coincidence but divine intervention. We were both meant to be there, standing at that exact location and sharing that exact same moment in time.*

I turned to Ron and said, "Now, is that not the most beautiful site you have ever witnessed?" Everything was moving in absolute perfect unison. The operations were clicking like a Rolex watch. We were both emotionally moved. We knew all the effort. We knew all the hours of practice and training to make this moment happen. We were both awestruck at the pure grandeur. Ron, aka Covey Leader, turned to me, a supernova gleam in his eyes, "Wolfpack, you are looking at pure, unadulterated passion! Just look at this. Incredible!"

I pointed at the ongoing example of what we believed was the epitome of earthmoving and replied, "Covey Leader, I have come to believe that passion is the driving force of all successful outcomes. Where there is no passion, there is no follow-through. But true passion unleashes a tidal wave of energy and focus that eventually leads to what was once perceived as unachievable results."

Covey Leader and/or Ron whirled around and exclaimed, "Damn, Lonnie, that is one hell of an awesome quote. You got to hold on to that one!"

I have carried it with me ever since.

Now, you can, too.

CHAPTER 17

THE POWER OF RECOGNITION— BUILDING & MAINTAINING HIGH MORALE

"Take time to appreciate employees, and they will reciprocate in a thousand ways."
—Bob Nelson

Recognition: To give "special notice or attention."[7] That is the good ol' *Merriam-Webster's Dictionary* at work again. I would like to add my own definition of recognition: "To acknowledge through the showing of appreciation." It's pretty damn simple and to the point.

---

7 "Recognition Definition & Meaning." Merriam-Webster. Accessed November 20, 2024. https://www.merriam-webster.com/dictionary/recognition.

Let's focus on two key phrases: "***Special notice*** and ***Showing appreciation.***" In my opinion and based on my 62 years of life experience, the word "recognition" is by far one of the most powerful words and can be an absolute Game-Changer in the outcome of events.

Recognition can lift you up. It can give you confidence and help you believe in yourself. Recognition will give you the strength and fortitude to carry on through what may seem like insurmountable odds. This word gives you unlimited power.

Recognition can actually be a life-changer. When you recognize somebody in a certain way or see their specific talents and abilities, that recognition helps them to believe in themselves. When you recognize their passion (oh, passion, there's that word again—I really love that word!) for what someone is doing, they look deep inside themselves and contemplate what you have just told them.

WHAT ELSE IS THERE?

Years ago, when I was a young grade setter, working my tail off so I could learn and become more, I knew I was supposed to *do more* with my life. I just wasn't sure what it was.

Thirty-five years ago, I would have never in a million years thought I would be where I am in my life today! But I believe the first step to here all started with recognition.

A great mentor of mine, an awesome blade hand named Bob Daniels, stopped me one day and yelled, "Morelock, jump up on this rig, and let's have a talk. I got somethin' to tell ya!"

I have shared about this impact on my life in past chapters, but it's worth sharing again!

I jumped up on the blade and said, "What you got, Ol' Smoothie?" That was my nickname for him, borne of my total and complete admiration of the man. Long before GPS, AGTEK, and Blade Control Systems, this guy was a master blade hand. He was one of the few operators my dad and grandpa would tell me about. A master of the trade. No other definition needed.

I can still hear their voices when I force myself to be quiet and pay attention. "Son, when a master talks to you, you listen." And I did.

Bob looked me right in the eye that day, a wry ol' grin on his leathered face, and said, "Lonnie, what you accomplish in this life is not going to matter. What is really going to matter is the positive impact you will have on those around you. That's what's gonna matter."

With a glow of love and recognition in his eyes, he barked, "Now, get off my blade, and get back to work."

I jumped off, went back to work, and all day long, I thought about what he said to me. I even thought about it on my drive home. Bob had bestowed on me a piece of spoken prophetic acknowledgment. The replay of this experience drives home the point I am trying to make. He was sharing recognition of my talent and ability that I couldn't even see.

I have carried his recognition of me and spoken on that fateful hot summer day so many years ago throughout my career. It has pushed me to perform at the highest levels possible. I cannot count the times on job sites when I have stopped and looked up into the deep blue sky and said, "Bob Daniels, hey, Ol' Smoothie, look at me now. Look at where I am today!"

Ol' Smoothie set me on my course with his heartfelt recognition on that life-changing day. He has been smoothing out the road for me every day since. When you truly recognize your people and when they truly understand that you admire them and what they are doing, you can change lives for the better.

Of all the components of "What Makes Your Team Tick?" I firmly believe recognition may be right at the top of the list!

All the factors in "What Makes Your Team Tick?" like aiming for Absolute Teamwork, Being a Leader, Knowing Your Role, Understanding Your Expectations, Knowing Your People, Effective Communication, Showing You Care, Training Your Team, Pursuing Continuous Improvement, Passion, and Motivation would never come together right without recognition.

Without recognition, there is no real success or achievement. It's comparable to spending weeks putting together a 1,000-piece puzzle but never finding that last, elusive piece, so you can never see the beautiful, finished product. Without recognition, you cannot enjoy the final taste of ultimate satisfaction.

As I try my best to thoroughly explain to you exactly what I am thinking, my mind immediately goes to gourmet cooking and the dishes my mom and grandma would create. I inherited their love of cooking, too.

Early in my childhood, I remember watching Mom and Grandma concoct extravagant meals that were so delectable I am drooling from the memories.

The special touches Mom and Grandma added to their recipes in their kitchen laboratories were the cause of these delicious sensations. These incredible, magnificent feasts, scrumptious meals, and desserts appeared from out of nowhere, and I would marvel as I watched them. They made their irresistible results seem so simple to produce. But I knew better. As I savored each dish placed in front of me, I wondered how they knew just the right amount of each ingredient to add to make their masterpieces.

OMG . . . could they cook. My Grandma could make a simple breakfast of bacon, eggs, and homemade biscuits taste like the greatest achievement of all time. All the while, she used the exact right ingredients and the exact right amount.

I was fascinated watching Mom and Grandma as they moved around their kitchens and sometimes questioned myself: *What if they didn't get it quite right? Would that ever happen?* These ladies were culinary geniuses, and I figured they could never make a mistake, or could they?

I often think of Mom and Grandma when I am cooking, and by far, one specific tip I have learned is that if I leave out one crucial ingredient or skip a critical part of the preparation process, the outcome is, to say the least, horrible. There's nothing like spending an entire day cooking a new dish, what I thought to be an off-the-charts recipe, only to have it end up in disaster because I screwed up and left out an essential element of what would have made it a very successful meal.

To bring this analogy home, remember, you may be the best leader on the planet and think you have one of the strongest, highest-performing teams of all time, but if you are not showing *special notice or appreciation* to every member of your team, then you truly have nothing.

Your team will not give you all they got without recognition. They will not go that extra mile to be their best. They won't help you shine like a supernova in the lens of the Hubble space telescope. You have not and will not achieve your team's full potential or your own if you leave out this key ingredient—the one that puts the icing on the cake—the Difference-Maker. Recognition. This simple word will take you and your teams places you have never gone before. You will experience the "Brick Wall Syndrome!"

EVERYTHING BUT THAT

One of my past client trainees never had any type of leadership training over his 30 years in the construction business. But I noticed on my first day on the job with him that one of his excavator operators was doing an outstanding job. Mind you, I had never met this operator before and knew nothing about him. But I did know a damn good excavation when I saw one, and this excavation was a work of art. The operator was executing flawlessly, and the excavation was beautiful.

> *I walked up to his rig and exclaimed, "Man, you are doing a great job. Your excavation is friggin' excellent!" He looked at me like I had three eyes, and I was momentarily perplexed.*

Shit, I just gave this guy a compliment. What gives??

I stared up at him and quietly asked, "What's the problem?" He lowered his head and replied, "Well, sir, no one has ever told me I was doing a good job. I've just never heard it before."

My jaw dropped. I said, "Are you shitting me?" (Yes, another Lonnieism.) I quickly recovered and said excitedly, "I mean . . . are you kidding me!?" He shook his head.

I stared him straight in the eye and said, "That's totally unacceptable. You are doing a great job, so I guess I am the first to tell you. Hopefully, you will hear that quite a bit more going forward. Get used to it."

In that instant, he became a kid in a candy store. I knew right then and there that this was Phase 1 of some definite changes that needed to be made with my new trainee.

Fueled with the fact that this man had never been recognized, I caught up with my trainee and nonchalantly asked him, "Ken, your excavator operator back there is one hell of a hand. You ever tell him he does a good job?"

"Hell no," Ken replied. "He knows it. I don't have to tell him."

RE EA EA EEEAAALLLALLY? The famous comedic exaggeration of Jim Carey in *Ace Venture Pet Detective* sprang to my mind. I laughed with gusto, and Ken turned around and gawked at me like I was losing my mind. Little did he know what I was thinking: "*Mr. Seasoned Manager Dude" is in desperate need of a serious education on the art of recognition.*

Now you might be thinking, *Lonnie, that really isn't that big of a deal.* But you know what? It *is* a big deal. In fact, it is a *huge* deal. And if you are not practicing showing people recognition, you are screwing up!

> *I believe that lack of recognition is one of the biggest problems in the construction industry, likely in any industry. We all suffer from not receiving and giving recognition.*

Let your people know that you actually care about them and give a damn about their performance and what they are doing for you every day. Tell them through your actions and words that you give a damn about their effort. Take a few seconds to give them a pat on the back or shake their hand and thank them for all they do. Show in some way that you are grateful for them and their abilities—for what they bring to the table.

When you see someone for their contributions, your recognition builds in that person, and it gives them and their team a never-ending desire to do more. It reinforces their confidence and character. Feeling appreciated inspires people to improve and drives them to become their level best.

Besides, we all like to be told we are doing a good job. It empowers us. So, pass it on!

The old-school mentality of believing "We can't tell a person they are doing a good job because they might slow down and not work as hard" is a load of bullshit. I wonder where that thought process even came from.

I have never had a direct report or team member slow down or show a lack of performance because I told them they were doing a great job. The response has always been and always will be the exact opposite. I note increased performance, better attitudes, improved morale, the willingness to take on more and do more, and to become what I call "Brick Wall Teams." As I said earlier, once these teams run through brick walls for you, they will ask, "Where's the next one?" All because they know in their hearts and minds that you care about them and are appreciative of their work, performance, and productivity.

Do it right, and they won't just hear you say it; they will feel it.

This simple ingredient, otherwise known as "gratitude," "appreciation," or "thankfulness," makes a gourmet meal so delicious.

APPRECIATION IN REAL LIFE

A couple of years ago, I was working for a new client. I knew right off that I would love working for this team. Most importantly, I knew in my heart that the CEO and president was a class act.

Nothing proved this more to me than one experience that, as I look back, defines everything I covered in the above paragraphs.

I was in the middle of training a new key foreman on a project one morning. The crews were working well together, and a lot was going on. This was a textbook high-production, wet utility underground pipe installation project, and the pipe laying work was being performed meticulously. The team was clicking along like a Rolex watch. I was helping the new foreman trainee with his Apple iPad and reviewing the project plans and work the team was doing when the CEO/president drove up, jumped out of his truck, and joined in the conversation and training. We were intently focused as we reviewed the project plans on the iPad.

The new foreman was making stellar progress in understanding the effectiveness of great organization and coordination, and that's what we were talking about. We finished up our training session, and I walked off to the ongoing operations with the new foreman. As I looked back, I noticed the CEO/president jump in his truck and drive off. I then watched in amazement as he drove out to the operations, got out of his truck, and jumped up on all the different machines to shake the hand of every single operator.

They talked briefly as the operators received pats on the back, and I saw the shine of admiration not only on the CEO's/president's face but on the faces of all the operators. This was one for the record books.

> *I was witnessing mutual gratitude, admiration, respect, and appreciation. It was absolutely beautiful.*

And he didn't stop there. This man then proceeded to walk around to every single laborer and did the exact same thing. Then he jumped back in his truck and drove off.

Incredible.

I knew immediately one of the reasons why he had such high-performing teams. He cared about and recognized his people. I felt this message in my soul.

Later, on my way home, I called him and told him how much what he did had impressed me. He didn't miss a beat. "They gotta know I care, Lonnie; they gotta know I appreciate their efforts."

This CEO/president got it. You want your team to perform. You want them to stick with you through thick and thin. You want them to run through brick walls for you. So . . . recognize them!

Nowadays, especially on LinkedIn, I read about companies having problems retaining their people. They wonder why they can't keep anyone in place. That's because . . .

Recognition Equals Retention

When I read these kinds of posts, I always think, *what kind of recognition program do they have? Do they ever just simply recognize their people's performance? Are they recognizing the efforts of the people working for them?*

I'm not talking about throwing a BBQ every few months or gifting swag now and then. I mean real, honest-to-God recognition that we all crave. Giving one-on-one recognition and acknowledgment for a job well done doesn't take much time, but it does so much. This recognition needs to be delivered DAILY! Not weekly, not monthly, and not once a year at an annual meeting. Commit to recognizing your people daily and watch your retention rates go up!

One of my favorite authors is the world-renowned leadership trainer, Ken Blanchard. His incredibly effective book, *The Heart of a Leader*, states, "If your team is not performing well, you might want to take a peek in the mirror." That is one awesome quote and so very, very true.

I want to take it one step further and ask, "If your team is not performing well, are you recognizing them? Are you recognizing your leaders? Are you recognizing your employees all the way down to the 'lowest' and newest hire apprentices or employees?"

Now, why did I include this last question and that particular word in quotes? Because they ARE NOT the lowest. No member of your company is the lowest. NONE.

Everyone plays an important role, no matter where they fall in the food chain. They are all important. They all need and want to be recognized. It really is that simple. Recognize a brand-new hire or first-step apprentice on their first day, and there is no telling what they might do or where they might go within your company. And they will know you appreciate their efforts on day one. That kind of appreciation makes people want to make things happen. Recognition incentivizes! Recognition breeds loyalty! Recognition causes your employees to want to be on your team and work for you. ***It breeds "the want."***

I don't mean sucking up; I am talking about REAL, heartfelt, honest recognition.

You want to know "What Makes Your Team Tick?" Give them recognition. Show them deep appreciation daily. Give them the "High-5," the "Fist Pump," "The Pat on the Back," the "Hey, Thank You Very Much," the "Wow, You Did a Friggin' Good Job Today!" and the "You Are Awesome!"

Whatever you say, leave them knowing you are full of love and respect for them and a job well done!

Let them eat, sleep, and breathe recognition, then sit back and watch the magic happen!

175

THE MASTER

A few months after I became a grading foreman, I had an awesome finish dozer hand working for me, operating a D9 Cat with a slope board. As we brought the massive cut slopes down, carving the guts out of the center of a mountain to make way for a new freeway expansion, his job was to cut and groom the slopes and finish them to the slope grade tolerances with the slope board.

If you have no idea what a slope board is, I will do my best to explain. It is a vertical steel extension, about 2 feet wide and 7-8 feet long, bolted to the side of the dozer blade. It has hydraulic functions, so it can move in and out and tilt at different angles. It also has serrated teeth for cutting the earth; operating it is almost like shaving your face but a lot more aggressive.

As the scrapers excavate the material from the cut, the slope board operator grooms the side of the cut slope, generally utilized on a 2:1 slope ratio, meaning for every two feet of horizontal distance on the slope, the slope drops one foot. A slope board operator is the crème de la crème of finish dozer operators. They have to be highly skilled, with a great eye for grade, and must be fast. There is no room for error, so they must be that good. As the cut comes down, the slope must come down at the same time, leaving the finished product behind. You can't climb back up and fix a mistake because the face of the excavated slope would be too steep.

Just imagine pulling a shaver across your bearded face and leaving a nice, smooth, shiny surface behind with no cuts or nicks. That is slope board operations at its finest.

The person on my crew at the helm of this role was Randy, and he was the best of the best. Nobody could run a slope board like he could.

Randy was a master.

Even though he was exceptional at his job, we never really clicked. I kept it to myself, but I thought he was an arrogant son-of-a-bitch. I don't know. Maybe he just didn't like me. I could live with that. I've learned in life that not everybody is going to like you. But, like my Dad always told me when it came to running crews, "Son, you don't have to eat Sunday dinner with them. You might not even like them. But if they are the best at what they do, work with them, not against them." I always took that message to heart and did my best to build working relationships with the more difficult individuals. Randy fit that bill.

Still, he was great at what he did, and I admired his talent and skill. Every chance I got, I told him, "Randy, you are the best damn slope board operator I have ever seen." It was true! I had seen and worked with quite a few, and he was the best of the best!

One early morning, before the shift started, Randy and I met up in the cut like we always did at that time. There we were on the steep hillside, talking about the battle plan with the goal of how much slope we wanted finished by the end of the day.

I would always tell him, "Damn, Randy, you can sure groom a slope. You create true works of art." And he would always answer back, "Morelock, shut the f___k up!"

Every time he said it, I was a little taken aback. What do you say to someone who constantly shoots down your kindness? My response was always a quiet, "Okay, then." Despite his reaction, I never relented with the recognition. I truly appreciated his work ethic and effort, and he needed to know it.

One morning, about 10:00 a.m., I jumped up on his Cat, perched on the side of the hill, to have a short conversation with him about future excavation plans. I wanted to punch a new haul road for the scrapers before lunch so we could start a new cut in the early afternoon. Randy's slope board expertise was required for this adventure because this new cut would be a steep, gnarly one, what we fondly referred to as having "pucker factor."

*This non-*Webster's Dictionary *definition comes directly from the field of earthmoving. The actual construction lingo definition is "Terrain that is so damn steep it will scare the hell of you and make your ass pucker up onto the seat, aka pucker factor."*

I looked at Randy and said, "Have you ever realized just how perfect your slopes really are?" He eyed me with an agitated scowl and exclaimed, "Lonnie, you know how tired I get of hearing you tell me how good I am?"

I whispered, all confused, "Really? Wow, that's a little weird!"

It took every measure of control I had not to lose it on him, but I kept my composure. I took off my super-cool, John Lennon-like sunglasses and said, "Randy, do me a favor. Get your ass off this Cat, and let's take a walk. Like right effing now!"

He gawked at me like, "Wwwhhaatt? Are you serious?"

Let me revert to Chapter 2—"Being the Leader": Always let them know when you are serious.

I could tell that Randy knew I was serious from the stone-cold expression on my face. Then I added words to remove any doubt: "I'm still the foreman on this spread, and I am asking you to do something, and that something is to come take a walk with me, so get your ass off that dozer."

Randy and I climbed off the dozer and walked up the bench we were currently working off of. I said, "Now take a good, hard, long look at that finish slope! Just stand here for a few minutes and study it!" We stood there in silence for a few minutes until he finally exclaimed, "What do you want me to see!?"

I quickly answered, "Randy, I want you to see absolute perfection. Do you realize that you groom that slope so perfectly that the teeth marks from your slope board—the grooves you are making—actually all line up with each other? I mean, how do you do that? You are the Michelangelo of slope board operators, and this is your Sistine Chapel. You are literally Leonardo De Vinci painting the Mona Lisa. Now, look at her. She is beautiful! It's scary-remarkable. You should be proud of your talent, your skill, your ability! I bet there are people down there, driving by on the freeway right now, looking up here and saying, 'Wow, how does that guy do that? Look at that slope. It's a work of art!'"

I exclaimed again, really punching the point home: "Look! Look with your own eyes! You are good. You are a master! Now, quit giving me shit about recognizing your talent. Enjoy it because everything I tell you is the absolute truth!"

Randy took a deep breath and glanced at me. I thought he was going to cry.

He quietly said, "Truth is, Lonnie, I've always had a real problem with being recognized and taking compliments. I grew up in a home with no one ever telling me I was good at anything."

I put my hand on his shoulder and said, "Randy, I know exactly where you're coming from. We have a lot in common. Hell, we might even be related, having grown up in the same homes. But put that negative shit behind you in the rearview mirror right where it belongs. Focus on how damn good you are now, the talent and ability that you truly have, and the unlimited recognition that you definitely deserve." Randy's eyes glowed with acknowledgment. I could see he was "picking up what I was throwing down," and he liked it.

I gave him a sly little grin and said, "Now, get your sorry ass back on that Cat, and let me see those grooves line up all the way to the bottom of this 200-foot cut! Your Mona Lisa is waiting for her painter."

Randy patted me fondly on the back and said, "Ya know, More-lock, you're alright. A bit of a pain in the ass, and you still piss me off all the time, but you're alright." He laughed as he walked away, then turned to look at me again just as he mounted the Cat, not bothering to hide the tears streaming down his face.

TEACHING KEN

Back to Ken, the "Seasoned Manager Dude," who had much to learn about the Power of Recognition. I spent the next eight weeks working with him on all aspects of "Being a Leader," with the focus on recognizing his team.

I encouraged Ken, time and time again, to shake an operator's hand or pat a laborer on the back and tell them they were doing a good job. At startup meetings in the morning, I urged him to recognize one individual for something good they had done the day before. At first, Ken struggled with this. It was foreign to him, like learning a new language.

Eventually, as he noted the positive response in his team and the light in their eyes when he gave them a well-deserved compliment, he started liking it. The guys definitely liked it. The change they experienced in Ken, although a bit odd at first, was breathtaking.

Soon, Ken noticed a change in his team. He saw additional effort being made throughout the shift. He couldn't ignore the new spring in their step or the morale and camaraderie building amongst the crew. The team worked together more efficiently and complimented each other on jobs well done.

A tidal wave of energy and enthusiasm was growing; both Ken and his team sensed it, and they loved it. At one of the last startup meetings I attended, Ken took the time to tell his team just how proud he was to be working with them and how much he appreciated all their efforts.

He said, "Guys, I know I have never been really good at this recognition thing, and I have wasted a lot of years with the wrong mindset. But the past is in the past. There's a new sheriff in town, and I just want you to know that I am damn proud to be your boss."

The applause was deafening.

I was even a bit overwhelmed by Ken's turnaround. Then, my little inner voice, which never fails me, whispered in my ear and said, "You are right where you are meant to be." I never feel more in alignment in my life than when I witness people choosing to be the best they can be.

When recognition is practiced diligently and correctly with high morale, camaraderie, Performance Above & Beyond, and Absolute Teamwork, your Team Will Always Tick!

CHAPTER 18

LET'S GET MOTIVATED

*"Coaches that can draw plays on a blackboard are a dime a dozen.
But the coaches that get into their players' heads and
motivate them are the winners."*
—Vince Lombardi

The whole "Let's Get Motivated" concept started at a very early age for me.

I remember trout fishing trips with my dad when we lived in Yreka, California. He worked as a heavy equipment operator for Gordon H. Ball, Inc., building a phase of the Interstate 5 Freeway through the Siskiyou Mountains. I absolutely loved Yreka, and the fishing was awesome. On the weekends, my dad would tell me, "Son, we are going to the Shasta River tomorrow morning to catch us some trout. You better be ready to get up early. Now, go get the fishing stuff ready to go!"

That was all I had to hear for my "Let's Get Motivated" energy to kick into high gear. Fishing poles and tackle boxes were speedily located, warm clothes were stacked up by my bed, the alarm clock was set, and the junk food lovingly placed in the cooler! Oh, yes! We were going fishing! I was on cloud nine, naturally!

Later, on those nights, his direction infused me with even more excitement—I knew what was coming. "Now get to bed. We got to get up real early. And we're gonna leave in the dark."

Oh, my God . . . leaving in the dark . . . going after the lunker rainbow. I could hardly contain myself. Getting motivated to sleep was a whole different story.

I learned quickly that when something phenomenal was about to happen, getting motivated was a breeze. Once I convinced myself to sleep, before I knew it, morning came. My alarm rang, and my dad bellowed from the kitchen, "Get movin', boy!" I sprang out of bed like a deer jumping over a fence, dressed in record time, and ran to the truck to load the gear—thoughts of ripping into a huge rainbow dancing in my head. The tingle of motivation rippled through my body. *I loved it*. "Let's do it, Dad! Let's go get 'em!" And off we went . . . .

Motivation made things happen.

Motivation started the ball rolling to the desired destination.

Motivation led to conquering the unconquerable. I learned it all started with an idea, a thought, or a plan and implementing every step needed to get to the desired conclusion.

I seemed to know, from the day I was born, that I would motivate people someday, somewhere down the road. My memories of the trout fishing trips rolled right into my early years in Little League. There I was, motivating the pitcher of our team; all the while, I sat on the bench, not playing. Instead of being bummed out, I thought *it's all good*.

I usually got in 3-4 great innings, and that was enough for me. On that bench, my mission was to relentlessly shout positive vibes to our pitcher. I saw it as my job to build him up and make him feel invincible. I remember yelling out at the team on the field and all the guys playing as I enthusiastically pushed them to be the best they could be. I can still close my eyes and see the third batter of the opposing team stepping up to the plate as I hollered encouragement to our pitcher, then "Strike three! You're out!" shouted the umpire. The pitcher looked over at me with a wide smile and gave me an arm pump, like, "Ya, Lonnie . . . we did this together!" I was totally convinced that my cheerleading from the bench was a Difference-Maker.

In high school sports, as I referenced, I perfected my motivational approaches for the teams I was on and built a following everywhere I went. Football games, basketball games, track and field, swim team . . . anywhere and everywhere my love of sports took me, my passion for motivating my team and teammates followed. I knew in my heart that positive motivation changed things for the better, even when we were getting our butts kicked. Was it always well received? Well, no, and sometimes, *definitely NO*. But that never fazed me.

The motivational wins far outweighed the motivational losses.

I was convinced that positive motivation was a direct driver of the eventual results. No question.

Although, I do vividly remember once when motivation got me in a lot of trouble.

I was a freshman playing on the JV football team, and we had just gotten whipped. Everyone was down and out and reeling from the tough loss.

I got up in the home team stands and excitedly watched the varsity team playing. *Damn, these guys were good.* They were undefeated, on a roll, and chasing the Small School Section Championship. I got caught up in the excitement and went into Motivation Mode, yelling and cheering on our football team, leading chants with the crowd—maybe even outdoing the cheerleading squad.

Then, some of my teammates showed up and started knocking me down. Their attitude was that I should be down in the dumps because of our loss. I remember thinking, *okay, so we lost, but we have another game next Friday. Let's get our asses ready for that one, and go get a win. And shouldn't we support our brethren, our varsity team, and do all we can to help them win?*

To my mind, this game wasn't about us. It was about them getting to the Small School Championship!

This moment may have been when I first learned that not all my motivation went over so well. But 99% of the time, it did. That was good enough for me!

If I have learned anything in my entire career and existence on this planet, it's that motivation is a driver. Motivation helps make things happen. It's how I came up with one of my famous bylines: "Make It Happen!" I have witnessed, time and time again, the power of motivation and how it can generate positive outcomes.

THE EPIPHANY

One day, while watching an NFL football game, an epiphany came over me. I could never recall watching the players come running out of the locker room onto the field, heads down, dejected, like they'd come from a funeral. HELL NO!

These players run out onto the field on fire, ready for battle, beating each other's shoulder pads and helmets. They get fired up to win!

How many professional fighters walk into the ring nonchalantly, exuding the vibe of "Oh well, just another day at the office"? Have you ever seen an absence of desire, drive, and emotion? These fighters are not dead inside, either. Boxers bound out into the auditorium, strutting their way to the ring, punching the air, talking shit to themselves and everyone around them.

Motivation is the driver. Motivation is the Formula 1 Race Car roaring down the track! Motivation is the enabler!

That passion inside you, that driving ambition to do all you can to be the best you can be, is what allows you to prevail against insurmountable odds. Use it, and you can do what everyone says cannot be done. You can literally achieve the impossible! It doesn't matter what it is, where it is, or how it is . . . . Motivation is a positive driver to a positive outcome. If it isn't, then why are some of the greatest achievers in history great motivators? Muhammed Ali, strutting to the ring time and time again, motivating himself that he is the best . . . and he was. Singing, "Float like a butterfly. Sting like a bee!" Tom Brady, constantly motivating himself and his teammates to win, win, win . . . *seven* Super Bowl rings later!

As I touched on in previous chapters, Coach Vince Lombardi motivated his players to be the absolute best they could be and is recognized as one of the greatest leaders in sports history. Ernest Shackleton motivated his entire shipwrecked crew across the Antarctic peninsula and through the frigid ice fields, bringing every single one of them to successful rescue—arguably, one of the greatest motivational leadership achievements of all time!

Great motivators change things. Great motivators make things happen. Great motivators are "Difference-Makers" in their lives and in the lives they touch. In my professional opinion, there is no denying this.

In the construction world, I have witnessed the effects positive motivation has on a project. I have, many times over, tasted the thrill of victory. On the flip side, I have also witnessed the heart-wrenching negative results stemming from a lack of motivation within a project team. I never want to see or feel that again—and there is no reason to.

As a leader, you must understand the motivational aspect of "What Makes Your Team Tick?"

WE ALL FIRE DIFFERENTLY

Every single construction team I have been involved with gets motivated differently. The secret sauce is figuring this out to understand what gets the team's blood pumping. You need to know: What turns them on? What amps them up? What makes them into a freight train steaming down the tracks?

As a new grading foreman in the dirt-moving world, I had no problem running all over the job site and getting everyone all lathered up! Of course, the continual focus on safety and quality was a given, but the actual building of the job was a different story. It was a blast, and I was getting paid very well to do it!

Every day, I was overwhelmed with how cool my job was. *Push more dirt with those big dozers! Move more dirt faster with those behemoth scrapers! Finish more subgrade with that beautiful 16G Blade and those 623 Paddlewheels, aka Paddle-Thumpers!*

My crew loved the drive of the earthmoving battle and how they changed the face of the Earth in record time. They enjoyed building private developments for future housing subdivisions, creating new freeways where two-lane highways used to be, and filling valleys for new dams to hold drinking water. We were all contributing to the future betterment of society. No matter the size, shape, or scope of the project . . . it was thrilling!

Then, when I took the step into salaried supervision, I quickly learned that project and operational motivation were needed to get to the next level. The tight margins on jobs, the striving to do more with less, the necessity to constantly achieve budgets, the manhours, and productivity requirements—it all needed a kick in the butt to ensure every goal was met. Motivation was serious business in a new way. Now, it was vitally important to the outcome.

Despite a deeper gravity and scope, I was determined to make motivation fun, desirable, and the go-to thought process in everyone's minds. I drummed into my crew's heads the motivation for safety, quality, productivity, and, most importantly, a successful outcome.

Anything less was unacceptable.

It was easy to talk about it, but putting it into action was another undertaking. I had to stop and ponder: *when it comes to motivating a team, how do we Make It Happen?* Throughout the years, I have discovered that the answer is relatively simple. In the famous words of Vince Lombardi, "Coaches that can draw plays on a blackboard are a dime a dozen, but the ones that get into their teammates' heads and motivate them are the winners." I am well aware that I shared this quote at the beginning of this chapter, but I want you to hear it again, the words echoing in your brain—that's how important it is!

With that in mind, I began to question the following:

Can high morale be taught?

Can enthusiasm and motivation become a work plan?

The answer was, and always will be, ABSOLUTELY!

Goals and achievements build morale.

Recognition builds morale.

The work plan then must include goals, achievement criteria, and recognition—all leading directly to motivation and higher morale.

Whether it is moving a specified quantity of cubic yards a day with Cats and scrapers or excavators and trucks, installing different types of underground piping, or laying and finishing road base for future paving operations—including paving roads or building walls for future structural concrete pours—installing electrical facilities for a future rapid transit train, bolting up mechanical parts for treatment plants, whatever the job happens to be—motivation for productivity is a must. Motivation for excellent performance is a must. Motivation for achievement is a must.

Motivation brings with it recognition. A simple pat on the back or "thank you" goes far. Recognizing the great daily performance of an operations team and calling out specific, outstanding individual performance can greatly increase a team member's confidence and give them the inner power and belief in themselves that they can achieve more. Recognizing the outstanding performance of a project team and instilling that feeling of pride and accomplishment combined with all of the above leads to ongoing positive motivation.

You wonder why people quit?

You wonder why a revolving door of employees leaves a company?

You wonder why top performers walk away?

You wonder why there is no feeling of teamwork and support for each other on a job site?

It is because there is no work plan for motivation or recognition. There is no lesson plan for teaching passion, enthusiasm, camaraderie, and teamwork. And it is such a simple recipe that is not so difficult to cook. All the key ingredients are available around you. Unfortunately, these key ingredients are not often used to the benefit of everybody involved.

MOTIVATING THE WHOLE CREW

Everyone on the crew, team, and project must be involved when you are motivating them. True involvement means everyone is looked upon as an integral part of the team's success. ***It means that everyone plays an essential role and is seen as adding value.*** Make sure each one of your people feels like their contribution is not only needed but that it is integral. No matter the job, the position, the discipline of work, or the level of their hierarchy . . . none of that matters. What truly matters is that every individual involved feels their participation is crucial. They all need to feel like they are essential and appreciated for the work they are doing for the team.

WHO CARES ABOUT TRUCK TICKETS?

I was on a mega-project years ago.

I had been sent to this particular project to assist with helping to bring this segment of the job to the finish line. There was lots of work left to do, and it was not going well. The history behind that is part of another story I won't get into here.

I had been on the job for about a week and was getting acclimated to it when I made it a mission to meet every single salaried staff team member and all the project's craft supervisors. At this point, everyone was still trying to figure out who I was, and I was in the same mode.

Remember, to motivate a team, a leader has to get to know each team member. You cannot know "What Makes Your Team Tick?" if you do not know your people. The problem was this team was definitely NOT ticking.

I truly thought I had met every member of the team, but there were quite a few, and it was a very large job with lots of project personnel.

I was making my way through one of the plethora of job trailers when I noticed a cubicle way in the back I had missed. I quietly walked back to this hidden compact area and stepped around the corner of the partition that separated the cubicle from the rest of the office trailer. A young man was sitting at his desk, pounding away at the keyboard. I stood there for a moment, quietly watching him go at it. He was totally focused and in his groove!

My movement must have caused him to look up, and he damn near jumped out of his chair, his eyes as wide as dinner plates. I couldn't help but crack up. That broke the ice, and I introduced myself, "Hi, my name is Lonnie Morelock. I am new to the project, and I am assisting the operations manager."

I put my hand out, and he nervously reached out to shake it, replying a little under his breath, "Uh, hi. My name is Chris."

"Well," I plastered a huge grin on my face, "how the hell are you, Chris? It's a pleasure to meet you!"

Chris just sat there, looking at me perplexed.

Do I stink? Why is he reacting this way? I know I put on deodorant and aftershave this morning. Chris softly replied, "I guess I am good."

> *"You guess!" I exclaimed, in my 10-personality-text-book-Lonnie-over-the-top fashion. "Damn, dude, you look great!"*

Chris was not loosening up.

So, what exactly is it that you do?" I asked, with an inquisitive expression on my face.

No response. Chris just kept looking at me like, "What gives?"

"Am I missing something here, or is there a problem?" I cautiously asked. He looked at me again like I was a space alien. He then said, "Well, Lonnie, um, um, nobody ever comes back here. I don't think I have seen anyone in my office in three weeks. I am kind of just left to myself."

My immediate response was, "Are you kidding me!?" I felt a storm of emotions overcome me—none of them good. "REALLY?!" I continued, immediately protective of Chris. "Why is that, and what exactly do you do?" Chris' initial response boiled my blood.

I get a little excited when I learn project personnel are not being treated right. Chris went on to explain that he took care of organizing and categorizing all the outside rent truck tickets from each day. His job was to compile all the tickets and keep track of the hours billed, etc. He told me he knew it wasn't a very glamorous job, and no one really paid any attention to him.

My heart fell a little at Chris's synopsis of himself and his role. I asked to take a look at his spreadsheet. It was AWESOME! I've always loved super-smart engineers with detailed spreadsheets. I am definitely not one of them.

In my serious manager voice, I told him, "Chris, let's go for a ride. Right now. Get up out of that chair, and let's take a drive through the project."

Chris' eyebrows about hit his hairline, and I thought he was going to have a stroke right there on the spot. He stammered, "Are you serious?"

I gave him a firm pat on the back and boomed, "Damn straight, I am. Let's go."

We strode out of the office, two men on a mission. Chris jumped in my way-cool company vehicle, a huge SUV I called THE TANK! It was plain from his bugging eyes and the thin line of his lips that he was overwhelmed. However, I was loving every minute of it.

I proceeded to drive Chris through the entire project, showing him all the different ongoing operations with outside rent dump trucks, aggregate trucks, off-haul highway trucks, and so on; the numbers were astounding. The cost of outside rental trucks on any project can be staggering. Being on top of daily truck tickets and recording hours of rent correctly can save a job enormous amounts of money. My goal was to help Chris see what he was truly responsible for. He was going to learn in a big hurry!

He was breathless. "Chris," I firmly explained, "you are tracking all of this. You have your pulse on hundreds of truckloads a day. All of these trucks are rentals and paid for by the hour. Do you know how important your job is?! Do you have any idea the cost per day associated with all the data you are so beautifully and precisely recording? You have a super important job. Never ever again question your involvement with this project team. You play a vitally important role."

Chris popped up in the seat, and I saw the first smile cross his face.

As I drove him back to the office, I asked him how he thought he could improve his current role. He gave me some great ideas, and I immediately initiated all of them.

194

After that pivotal drive, I made a point to check in with Chris several times a week. His motivation for his job had gone through the roof. He had built a detailed tracking system that he put together on the wall in his office. I instructed him to drive the job once a day to make sure he wasn't missing any of the operations. I also gave him additional responsibilities.

The result and change in Chris were remarkable. He was on fire to track every single rental truck for every single hour on the job.

The moral of this story is that simply taking the time to show a member of your team just how important they are, no matter the role they play, is a self-motivator. Motivation does not always mean hype and noise, pomp and circumstance, hollering and cheerleading. It can simply be a product of showing that you sincerely care about who is working for you and the efforts they put forth for the good of the team. Above all, it is about people *knowing* that you really and truly care.

Finding out what makes each member of a team tick is not rocket science. To learn this vital fact that will change everything in your leadership, all you have to do is take the time to learn about, understand, and involve them. Your next step is to uncover what motivates them. Every individual is different. Everyone gets motivated in a different way. Make sure you do the work to figure out these differences—that will make all the difference!

Take the time to care about, understand, and empower every member of your team—to discover their passion and inner drive. When you learn this, you will learn how to motivate them.

Then the Saturn V rockets will launch! . . . and you will have learned, "What Makes Your Team Tick?"

NOW, GO . . . . MAKE IT HAPPEN!

ACKNOWLEDGMENTS

First and foremost, my Lord and Savior Jesus Christ and my Father, God, in Heaven, your Word is so true. You are the guiding light in my life, and you have, without a doubt, given me "blessings for ashes."

Second, to my family: Your love, selfless support, and never-ending belief in me have been instrumental in getting me to this most blessed place in my life.

To my wonderful, incredible wife, Michelle, my Pooh: You have taught me what true love really means, and I am so very grateful and thankful for all your love, support, and tireless encouragement. You are my *Notebook*, and we will continue our journey together into eternity.

To my family: You are all I could have ever asked for, and I love you all with all my heart.

My mom: Teddie McGregor
My dad: George Morelock
My stepdad: Gene McGregor
My grandpa: Max Morelock
My grandma: Cena Mae Morelock
My aunt: "Hootie" Lathrop
My uncle: Al Lathrop

My uncle: Bob Graham
My daughter: Michelle Marman
My daughter: Amanda Geller
My brothers: Rod Hall, Henry Souza, Dan Dinsdale, Rob Parish, Jay Selby, Mike Pauletto, Isaac Garcia, Lucas Camp, and Zack Baldwin
My little sister: Stephanie Verdon Fuller

To my publisher and now close friend, Hilary Jastram, I would never have gotten here without you. Your monumental efforts in guiding me every step of the way through this book writing process and instilling in me the confidence to believe in myself as a writer have all helped to make this dream come true.

To my mentors, colleagues, and friends—over my 40+ year career, this list is truly endless. You have all been such a huge factor in my life, in your own special way and in helping me navigate my successful construction and leadership career. There are not enough words in *Webster's Dictionary* to describe and explain my gratitude for all you have done for me over the years. You have positively impacted a man who appreciates it more than you could ever know. My admiration, honor, and respect for you can never be measured.

Bob Daniels	Gary Chapman
Herman Hall	Richard Raine
Larry Bunning	Barry Pihowich
Sam Vassey	John Jansen
Bob Settlage	Mike Phelps
Val Peterson	Rod Morton
Frank Haser	Dave Hazen
Bob Stoddard	Todd Orbus
Larry Sisk	Chris Wiese
Tom Sievwright	Lance Regular
"Big" Jim Mora	Mark Wheeler
Tracie Mayes	Lester Smith

Chris Hanna
Dennis Leonard
John Manes
Pete Remington
John Watson
Tom Trimble
Laura Hernandez
Kevin Freeman
Mary Oatman
Jim Eisenhart
Jon Swartzentruber

Manuel de Freitas
Danny Campiotti
David Brown
Stephanie Ottovan
Tony Zandridad
Sue-Weiler Doke
Jake Weaver
Tom Schmidt
Pat Lazansky
Shannon Buell
Farshad Mazloom

For those I may have forgotten to list, you will never be forgotten in my heart.

ABOUT THE AUTHOR

Lonnie Morelock grew up in a construction family and was introduced to the industry at an early age. He took his first ride on a Cat 651 Scraper with his dad when he was five years old and has been "hooked" on heavy construction ever since.

In 1980, at 18 years old, right out of high school, Lonnie joined the Operating Engineers Local Union #3 on the Warm Springs Dam (now Lake Sonoma) Project in Healdsburg, California. For the next 20 years, he honed his skills as a heavy equipment operator, working on a plethora of civil grading projects for multiple companies throughout Northern California and Alaska.

In 1992, Lonnie took a job as a grade setter with Kiewit Pacific Company in Brisbane, California. Through his strong work ethic and civil grading knowledge, Lonnie was soon promoted to a grading foreman position, supervising mass grading crews for Kiewit on large-scale civil grading projects.

In 1996, Lonnie was promoted to general excavation foreman on the Los Vaqueros Earth-Fill Dam Project in Brentwood, California.

In 2000, the Kiewit Companies offered Lonnie a salaried superintendent position, which he accepted with unbridled enthusiasm and never looked back. He quickly rose through the ranks, managing large, heavy civil projects throughout Northern California.

In 2008, Kiewit promoted Lonnie to project manager on Phase 1 of the Folsom Dam Auxiliary Spillway Flood Control Project for the Bureau of Reclamation. This project was very successful, earning Kiewit the Bureau of Reclamation's "Construction Safety Award for 2008." Lonnie was nominated for the coveted Peter Kiewit—Excellence in Management Award for his team's efforts.

In the fall of 2010, Kiewit sent Lonnie to his first mega-project assignment as the operations manager of Segment 4 on the Port Mann Highway 1 Project in Vancouver, British Columbia. It was on this job that Lonnie truly developed his motivational communication and team-building skills as he improved his own distinct methods for training field supervisors. Working with individuals under his immediate supervision, he soon realized that developing supervisors into field leaders proficient in team building and team performance was his true calling. Lonnie went on to build high-performing teams on large-scale construction projects throughout the Western United States.

Lonnie ended his successful Kiewit career in 2018 as site logistical operations manager on the Oroville Dam Emergency Spillway Project in Northern California. Once retired from Kiewit, he followed his passion and started Morelock Motivational, Inc., focusing on what he learned throughout his entire construction career: training leadership skills, with an emphasis on productivity, continuous improvement, and his passion for building high-performance teams.

Lonnie resides in Rocklin, California, with his wife, Michelle, and their four dogs, Bodie, Red, Gracie, and Lu Lu.

DISCLAIMER

This book is a truthful recollection of actual events in the author's life. The events, places, and conversations in this book have been recreated from memory. The names and details of some individuals or entities have been changed to respect their privacy.

The information provided within this book is for general informational, educational, and entertainment purposes only. The author and publisher are not offering such information as business, investment or legal advice, or any other kind of professional advice, and the advice and ideas contained herein may not be suitable for your situation.

Any use of the information provided within this book is at your own risk, and it is provided without any express or implied warranties or guarantees on the part of the author or publisher. No warranty may be created or extended by sales representatives or written sales materials. You should seek the services of a competent professional before beginning any business endeavor or investment.

Neither the author nor the publisher shall be held liable or responsible to any person or entity with respect to any financial, commercial, or other loss or damages (including but not limited to special, incidental, or consequential damages) caused or alleged to have been caused, directly or indirectly, by the use of any of the information contained herein.

www.ingramcontent.com/pod-product-compliance
Lightning Source LLC
Chambersburg PA
CBHW070819120626
46556CB00002B/580